EASY
PEASY
MEALS

EASY
PEASY
MEALS

PAVILION

This edition published in the United Kingdom
in 2015 by
Pavilion
1 Gower Street
London
WC1E 6HD

The Good Housekeeping website is
www.goodhousekeeping.co.uk

10 9 8 7 6 5 4 3 2

ISBN 978-1-908449-93-1

A catalogue record for this book is available from
the British Library.

Reproduction by Dot Gradations Ltd, UK
Printed and bound by
Time Printing Ltd, Malaysia

This book can be ordered direct from the publisher
at www.pavilionbooks.com

NOTES

Both metric and imperial measures are given for
the recipes. Follow either set of measures, not a
mixture of both, as they are not interchangeable.

All spoon measures are level.
1 tsp = 5ml spoon; 1 tbsp = 15ml spoon.

Ovens and grills must be preheated to the specified
temperature.

Medium eggs should be used except where
otherwise specified. Free-range eggs are
recommended.

Note that some recipes contain raw or lightly
cooked eggs. The young, elderly, pregnant women
and anyone with an immune-deficiency disease
should avoid these because of the slight risk
of salmonella.

Contents

Storecupboard Suppers

The Well-stocked Storecupboard

A well-stocked storecupboard can help you rustle up a quick meal at short notice. However, resist the urge to fill the cupboard with interesting bottles that you 'might use one day'.

Stocking your storecupboard

Dried

- ❑ Pasta and noodles
- ❑ Rice (long-grain, Arborio and other risotto rice, pudding rice)
- ❑ Pulses
- ❑ Pizza bases
- ❑ Nuts (pinenuts, walnuts, almonds)
- ❑ Dried fruits
- ❑ Stock cubes
- ❑ Spices and herbs
- ❑ Salt and ground black pepper
- ❑ Flour (plain, self-raising, wholemeal and cornflour)
- ❑ Dried yeast
- ❑ Gelatine
- ❑ Baking powder, cream of tartar, bicarbonate of soda
- ❑ Sugar
- ❑ Tea
- ❑ Coffee
- ❑ Cocoa powder

Bottles and jars

- ❑ Mayonnaise
- ❑ Tomato ketchup and purée
- ❑ Tabasco sauce
- ❑ Worcestershire sauce
- ❑ Sweet chilli sauce
- ❑ Pasta sauces
- ❑ Thai fish sauce
- ❑ Curry paste
- ❑ Chutneys
- ❑ Pickles
- ❑ Olives
- ❑ Capers
- ❑ Mustards
- ❑ Oils
- ❑ Vinegar
- ❑ Jam
- ❑ Marmalade
- ❑ Honey

Cans

- ☐ Chopped and whole tomatoes
- ☐ Fish (salmon, tuna, anchovies)
- ☐ Beans, chickpeas and lentils
- ☐ Coconut milk/cream
- ☐ Fruits

Variations

- Use 100g (3½oz) sun-dried tomatoes instead of the new potatoes.
- Throw in a handful of halved pitted black olives as you pour the egg into the pan.

Storecupboard Recipes

Storecupboard Omelette

A drizzle of olive oil or knob of butter, 1 large onion, finely chopped, 225g (8oz) cooked new potatoes, sliced, 125g (4oz) frozen petit pois, thawed, 6 medium eggs, beaten, 150g pack soft goat's cheese, sliced, salt and ground black pepper.

1 Heat the oil or butter in a 25.5cm (10in) non-stick, ovenproof frying pan. Add the onion and fry for 6–8 minutes until golden. Add the potatoes and petit pois and cook, stirring, for 2–3 minutes. Preheat the grill.

2 Spread the mixture over the base of the pan and pour in the eggs. Tilt the pan to coat the base with egg. Leave the omelette to cook undisturbed for 2–3 minutes, then top with the cheese.

3 Put the pan under the hot grill for 1–2 minutes until the egg is just set (no longer, or it will turn rubbery) and the cheese starts to turn golden. Season with salt and pepper and serve immediately.

Mixed Beans with Lemon Vinaigrette

400g can mixed beans, drained and rinsed, 400g can chickpeas, drained and rinsed, 2 shallots, finely sliced, 6 fresh mint sprigs and grated lemon zest to garnish

For the lemon vinaigrette

Juice of 1 lemon, 2 tsp runny honey, 8 tbsp extra virgin olive oil, 3 tbsp freshly chopped mint, 4 tbsp roughly chopped flat-leafed parsley, salt and freshly ground black pepper.

1 Put the beans, chickpeas and shallots into a large bowl.
2 To make the lemon vinaigrette, whisk together the lemon juice, honey and seasoning. Gradually whisk in the oil and stir in the chopped herbs.
3 Pour the vinaigrette over the bean mixture, toss well, then garnish with the mint sprigs and lemon zest and serve.

Perfect Eggs
Cracking and separating

Some recipes call for eggs to be separated into whites and yolks. It's easy, but it requires care. If you're separating more than one egg, break each one into an individual bowl or cup. Separating them individually means that if you break one yolk, you won't spoil the whole batch. Keeping the whites yolk-free is particularly important for techniques such as whisking.

1 Crack the egg sharply and carefully, right in the middle, to make a break between the two halves that is just wide enough to get your thumbnail into.
2 Holding the egg over a bowl with the ends downwards, carefully separate the halves. Some of the white will drip and slide into the bowl while the yolk sits in the end of the shell.
3 Carefully slide the yolk into the other end, then back again, to allow the remaining white to drop into the bowl. Take care not to break the yolk; even a speck can stop the whites from whisking up.

Eggs are a wonderfully versatile ingredient; they are used in a wide range of hot and cold desserts, from soufflés and meringues to pancakes and custards.

Pancakes

To make eight pancakes, you will need:

125g (4oz) plain flour, a pinch of salt, 1 medium egg, 300ml (½ pint) milk, oil and butter to fry.

1. Sift the flour and salt into a bowl, make a well in the centre and whisk in the egg. Gradually beat in the milk to make a smooth batter, then leave to stand for 20 minutes.

2. Heat a heavy-based frying pan and coat lightly with fat. Pour in a little batter and tilt the pan to coat the base thinly and evenly.

3. Cook over a moderately high heat for 1 minute or until golden. Turn carefully and cook the other side for 30 seconds to 1 minute.

Cheesy Chicken and Vegetable Cobbler

Hands-on time: 20 minutes
Cooking time: about 20 minutes

200g (7oz) cooked skinless chicken breast, cut into bite-size pieces

200g (7oz) frozen mixed vegetables

300g can cream of tomato soup

175g (6oz) self-raising flour, plus extra to dust

½ tbsp baking powder

50g (2oz) mature Cheddar, grated

75ml (3fl oz) milk, plus extra to brush

1 medium egg, lightly beaten

½ tbsp vegetable oil

salt and freshly ground black pepper

1 Preheat the oven to 200°C (180°C fan oven) mark 6. In a medium bowl, stir together the cooked chicken, frozen vegetables, soup and some seasoning. Pour the mixture into a 1 litre (1¾ pint) shallow ovenproof dish and put to one side.

2 Sift the flour, baking powder and a large pinch of salt into a large bowl. Stir in most of the cheese. Beat the milk, egg and oil together in a separate bowl.

3 Pour the milk mixture into the flour bowl and use a cutlery knife to bring it together until the dough forms clumps. Add a splash of milk if it looks too dry.

4 Tip the dough on to a lightly floured worksurface and pat it into a rough 9cm × 15cm (3½in × 6in) rectangle. Cut the rectangle into eight equal squares, then arrange the scones on top of the chicken mixture. Brush each scone with a little milk, then sprinkle over the remaining cheese.

5 Cook for 20 minutes or until the scones are risen and golden, and the filling is bubbling and piping hot. Serve immediately.

Serves 4

Quorn Lasagne

Hands-on time: 25 minutes
Cooking time: about 1 hour

3 tbsp olive oil

1 onion, finely chopped

2 × 300g bags frozen Quorn mince

100ml (3½fl oz) red wine

2 × 400g cans chopped tomatoes

1½ tbsp mixed dried herbs

½ vegetable stock cube

4 tbsp plain flour

600ml (1 pint) milk

9 dried and ready-to-cook lasagne sheets

50g (2oz) mature Cheddar, grated

salt and freshly ground black pepper

salad to serve

1 Heat 1 tbsp of the oil in a large pan and fry the onion for 10 minutes until softened. Turn up the heat, add the Quorn and fry for 5 minutes until golden. Add the wine and simmer for 5 minutes.

2 Stir in the tomatoes and mixed herbs, then crumble in the stock cube and some seasoning. Bring to the boil, reduce the heat and simmer for 5 minutes until thick. Take off the heat.

3 Next make the white sauce. Heat the remaining oil in a small pan and stir in the flour. Cook for 30 seconds, then take off the heat and gradually whisk in the milk. Put the milk mixture back on to the heat. Bring to the boil, reduce the heat and simmer for 5 minutes, whisking, until thick and glossy.

4 Preheat the oven to 200°C (180°C fan oven) mark 6. Spoon a third of the mince mixture into the base of a 2 litre (3½ pint) ovenproof dish. Cover with three lasagne sheets and a little white sauce. Repeat the layering process twice more, finishing with a layer of white sauce. Sprinkle over the cheese and cook for 30–35 minutes until bubbling and golden (cover with foil if browning too quickly). Serve immediately with a salad.

Serves 6

Salmon and Pea Fishcakes

Hands-on time: 15 minutes
Cooking time: about 10 minutes

100g (3½oz) frozen peas

15 cream crackers, about 125g (4oz)

2 × 180g cans skinless and boneless
  salmon, drained

1 medium egg, separated

a few drops Tabasco, to taste

1 tbsp freshly chopped dill

1 tbsp vegetable oil

3 tbsp mayonnaise

2 tbsp sweet chilli sauce

salt and freshly ground black pepper

green salad to serve

1 Put the peas into a bowl, cover them
  with boiling water and leave for a few
  minutes. Meanwhile, put five of the
  cream crackers into a food processor
  and whiz until fine. Tip the cracker
  crumbs on to a shallow plate and put
  to one side for the coating.

2 Whiz the remaining whole crackers
  until fine. Add the salmon, egg yolk,
  Tabasco, dill and plenty of seasoning
  to the processor and whiz again until
  combined. Drain the peas and add to
  the salmon mixture, then pulse briefly
  to combine.

3 Put the egg white into a shallow bowl
  and whisk lightly with a fork to break
  it up. Shape the salmon mixture
  into four patties, dip each into the
  egg white, then coat in the reserved
  cracker crumbs.

4 Heat the oil in a large frying pan and
  cook the fishcakes for about 5 minutes
  on each side until they are golden and
  piping hot.

5 Meanwhile, stir the mayonnaise and
  sweet chilli sauce together in a small
  bowl. Serve the fishcakes with the
  dipping sauce and a green salad.

Serves 4

Penne Puttanesca

Hand-on time: 15 minutes
Cooking time: about 25 minutes

350g (12oz) dried penne pasta

1 tbsp olive oil

1 onion, finely chopped

400g can chopped tomatoes

2 tsp dried oregano

120g can boneless and skinless sardine
fillets, drained

50g (2oz) black olives, pitted

a small handful of curly parsley,
chopped

salt and freshly ground black pepper

SAVE EFFORT

Anchovies are the classic addition
to this dish for their salty oomph,
but sardines will give it more
substance and texture.

1 Bring a large pan of salted water to the boil and cook the pasta according to the pack instructions. Drain well, keeping a cupful of the cooking water to one side.

2 Meanwhile, heat the oil in a large pan and fry the onion for 10 minutes until softened but not coloured. Add the tomatoes and oregano, then bring the mixture to the boil, reduce the heat and simmer for 15 minutes until thickened. Stir in the sardines and olives – the stirring should help break up the fish slightly.

3 Add the pasta to the sauce and toss well to combine. Add a little of the pasta water if the mixture looks too dry. Check the seasoning, then divide among four bowls. Garnish with parsley and serve immediately.

Serves 4

Paella

Hands-on time: 15 minutes
Cooking time: about 35 minutes

1 tbsp vegetable oil

1 large onion, thinly sliced

4 skinless chicken thigh fillets, roughly chopped

2 garlic cloves, finely chopped

¼ tsp paprika

½ tsp turmeric or a large pinch of saffron

300g (11oz) risotto or paella rice

1 litre (1¾ pint) chicken stock

100g (3½oz) roasted red peppers from a jar, seeded and roughly chopped

a small handful of fresh flat-leaf parsley, roughly chopped

salt and freshly ground black pepper

1 Heat the oil in a large frying pan and fry the onion for 10 minutes or until softened. Add the chicken and fry for 3 minutes over a high heat until beginning to colour. Stir in the garlic, paprika and turmeric or saffron and cook for 1 minute more.

2 Add the rice to the pan, then pour over the stock and leave it to simmer gently for 20–25 minutes, stirring occasionally, until the rice is tender and cooked through. Stir in the peppers. Check the seasoning, then scatter over the parsley. Serve immediately.

SAVE MONEY

This versatile rice dish easily adapts to suit what's in your fridge – add any leftover veg or cooked meat you like to give it extra flavour.

Serves 4

Sticky Ribs with Rice and Beans

Hands-on time: 15 minutes
Cooking time: about 55 minutes

125g (4oz) tomato ketchup

1½ tbsp soy sauce

1½ tbsp white wine vinegar

3 tbsp honey

1½ tsp mixed spice

½ tsp hot chilli powder

1.5kg (3¼lb) individual pork spare ribs

250g (9oz) basmati rice

400g can kidney beans, drained and rinsed

a large handful of fresh coriander, chopped

green salad to serve

1 Preheat the oven to 200°C (180°C fan oven) mark 6. Line a large roasting tin with a double layer of foil. In a large bowl, mix together the tomato ketchup, soy sauce, white wine vinegar, honey, mixed spice and chilli powder. Add the ribs to the bowl and stir to coat completely, then empty the ribs and glaze into the lined roasting tin and spread out evenly.

2 Cover with foil and cook for 20 minutes. Uncover, then turn the ribs and put them back into the oven for 30–35 minutes, turning in the glaze occasionally, until they're dark and sticky (most of the liquid should have evaporated).

3 Cook the rice according to the pack instructions, adding the kidney beans for the final 2 minutes of cooking. Drain and stir in the coriander. Serve the rice with the ribs and a salad.

SAVE TIME

Make the glaze in advance for up to 5 hours, add the ribs and store in the fridge until ready to cook. This glaze would be fantastic on grilled sausages or sizzling pork, too.

22

Serves 4

Quick and
Easy Classics

Classic Omelette

TAKE
5

Hands-on time: 5 minutes
Cooking time: 5 minutes

2–3 medium eggs

1 tbsp milk or water

25g (1oz) unsalted butter

salt and freshly ground black pepper

green salad to serve

1 Whisk the eggs in a bowl, just enough to break them down – over-beating spoils the texture of the omelette. Season with salt and ground black pepper, and add the milk or water.

2 Heat the butter in an 18cm (7in) omelette pan or non-stick frying pan until it is foaming, but not brown. Add the eggs and stir gently with a fork or wooden spatula, drawing the mixture from the sides to the centre as it sets and letting the liquid egg in the centre run to the sides. When set, stop stirring and cook for 30 seconds or until the omelette is golden brown underneath and still creamy on top: don't overcook. If you are making a filled omelette, add the filling at this point.

3 Tilt the pan away from you slightly and use a palette knife to fold over one-third of the omelette to the centre, then fold over the opposite third. Slide the omelette out on to a warmed plate, letting it flip over so that the folded sides are underneath. Serve immediately with a green salad.

Perfect Pasta

Perfectly cooked pasta can be a super-quick accompaniment or a meal in itself. Whether you are cooking dried or fresh pasta, follow these simple steps, then add an easy pasta sauce for a meal in minutes.

Cooking pasta

There are a number of mistaken ideas about cooking pasta, such as adding oil to the water, adding salt only at a certain point and rinsing the pasta after cooking. The basics couldn't be simpler. Filled pasta is the only type of pasta that needs oil in the cooking water – the oil reduces friction, which could tear the wrappers and allow the filling to come out. Use 1 tbsp for a large pan of water. Rinse the pasta after cooking only if you are going to cool it to use in a salad.

Dried pasta

1   Heat the water with about 1 tsp salt per 100g (3½oz) of pasta. Bring to a rolling boil, then add all the pasta and stir well for 30 seconds, to keep the pasta from sticking.

2   Once the water is boiling again, set the timer for 2 minutes less than the cooking time on the pack and cook uncovered.

3   Check the pasta when the timer goes off, then every 60 seconds until it is cooked al dente: tender, but with a slight bite at the centre. Drain in a colander.

Fresh pasta

Fresh pasta is cooked in the same way as dried, but for a shorter time. Bring the water to the boil. Add the pasta to the boiling water all at once and stir well. Set the timer for 2 minutes and keep testing every 30 seconds until the pasta is cooked al dente: tender, but with a little bite at the centre. Drain in a colander.

How much pasta do I need?

Allow 75g (3oz) dried pasta shapes or noodles or 125g (4oz) fresh or filled pasta shapes per person. Cook the pasta until al dente: tender, but with a little bite at the centre. Follow the timings on the pack and start testing 1 minute before the recommended time. The pasta will continue to cook a little after draining.

Smoked Haddock Kedgeree

Hands-on time: 10 minutes
Cooking time: 20 minutes

175g (6oz) long-grain rice
450g (1lb) smoked haddock fillets
2 medium eggs, hard-boiled and shelled
75g (3oz) butter
salt and cayenne pepper
freshly chopped flat-leafed parsley
  to garnish

1 Cook the rice in a pan of lightly salted fast-boiling water until tender. Drain well and rinse under cold running water.

2 Meanwhile, put the haddock into a large frying pan with just enough water to cover. Bring to simmering point, then simmer for 10–15 minutes until tender. Drain, skin and flake the fish, discarding the bones.

3 Chop one egg and slice the other into rings. Melt the butter in a pan, add the cooked rice, fish, chopped egg, salt and cayenne pepper and stir over a medium heat for 5 minutes or until hot. Pile on to a warmed serving dish and garnish with the sliced egg and chopped parsley.

Serves 4

Speedy Chicken Pilaf

Hands-on time: 5 minutes
Cooking time: about 20 minutes

1 tbsp oil

1 onion, finely sliced

1 tbsp balti curry paste

6 skinless chicken thigh fillets, cut into finger-size strips

2 × 250g pouches pre-cooked rice

150g (5oz) peas

100g (3½oz) spinach

2 tbsp mango chutney, plus extra to serve

flaked almonds (optional)

salt and freshly ground black pepper

1 Heat the oil in a large pan over a medium heat. Add the onion and fry for 5 minutes until beginning to soften. Stir in the curry paste and cook for 1 minute, then add the chicken and fry for 8 minutes until cooked through. Add a splash of water if the pan looks dry.

2 Stir in the rice, peas and 100ml (3½fl oz) water, then cook for 3 minutes until the rice is fully tender. Stir through the spinach and chutney, then check the seasoning. Scatter with almonds, if you like and serve with some extra mango chutney on the side.

Serves 4

Tomato, Prawn and Garlic

Put 350g (12oz) cooked peeled prawns into a bowl with 4 tbsp sun-dried tomato paste and stir well. Heat 1 tbsp olive oil and 15g (½oz) butter in a frying pan. Gently cook 3 sliced garlic cloves until golden. Add 4 large chopped tomatoes and 125ml (4fl oz) dry white wine. Leave the sauce to bubble for about 5 minutes, then stir in the prawns and 20g (¾oz) freshly chopped flat-leafed parsley.

Creamy Pesto

Put 5 tbsp freshly grated Parmesan, 25g (1oz) toasted pinenuts, 200g carton low-fat fromage frais and 2 garlic cloves into a food processor. Whiz to a thick paste. Season generously with salt and ground black pepper. Add 40g (1½oz) each torn fresh basil leaves and roughly chopped flat-leafed parsley and whiz for 2–3 seconds.

Walnut and Creamy Blue Cheese

Heat 1 tsp olive oil in a small pan, add 1 crushed garlic clove and 25g (1oz) toasted walnut pieces and cook for 1 minute – the garlic should just be golden. Add 100g (3½oz) cubed Gorgonzola and 150ml (¼ pint) single cream. Season with ground black pepper.

Lemon and Parmesan

Cook pasta shells in a large pan of boiling salted water for the time stated on the pack. Add 125g (4oz) frozen petit pois to the pasta water for the last 5 minutes of the cooking time. Drain the pasta and peas, put back in the pan and add the grated zest and juice of ½ lemon and 75g (3oz) freshly grated Parmesan. Season with ground black pepper, toss and serve immediately.

Mushroom and Cream

Heat 1 tbsp olive oil in a large pan and fry 1 finely chopped onion for 7–10 minutes until soft. Add 300g (11oz) sliced mushrooms and cook for 3–4 minutes. Pour in 125ml (4fl oz) dry white wine and bubble for 1 minute, then stir in 500ml (18fl oz) low-fat crème fraîche. Heat until bubbling, then stir in 2 tbsp chopped tarragon. Season with salt and ground black pepper.

Gnocchi Bake

Hands-on time: 5 minutes
Cooking time: about 10 minutes

750g (1lb 11oz) gnocchi

3 tbsp mascarpone cheese

400g can cherry tomatoes

½ tbsp sun-dried tomato purée

1 spring onion, thinly sliced

½ garlic clove, finely chopped

125g ball buffalo mozzarella, torn
  into pieces

salt and freshly ground black pepper

a large handful of rocket to garnish

1 Preheat the grill to medium. Cook the gnocchi in a large pan of lightly salted boiling water for 3–4 minutes or until they float to the surface. Drain well and tip the gnocchi into a large bowl.

2 Stir through the mascarpone, tomatoes, tomato purée, spring onion and garlic. Check the seasoning, then transfer the mixture to a 2 litre (3½ pint) ovenproof casserole dish. Dot over the mozzarella, then put under the grill for 5 minutes or until piping hot and golden. Garnish with rocket and serve.

Cheat's Macaroni Cheese

Hands-on time: 10 minutes
Cooking time: about 10 minutes

300g (11oz) dried macaroni

300g pack cauliflower and broccoli
florets (or ½ small head each
broccoli and cauliflower), cut
into smaller florets

300g (11oz) low-fat cream cheese

150g (5oz) mature Cheddar, grated

½ tsp English mustard

1 tbsp freshly chopped chives, plus extra
to garnish

25g (1oz) dried breadcrumbs

salt and freshly ground black pepper

green salad to serve

1 Bring a large pan of water to the boil
and cook the pasta according to the
pack instructions. Add the vegetables
for the last 3 minutes. Drain and put
back into the pan.

2 Meanwhile, put the cream cheese and
most of the Cheddar into a small pan
and heat gently to melt, then stir in
the mustard, chives and some salt and
ground black pepper. Stir the sauce
into the drained pasta pan and check
the seasoning. Add a little water if you
like a thinner sauce.

3 Preheat the grill to medium. Divide
the macaroni mixture among four
individual heatproof dishes, then put
them on a baking sheet. Sprinkle the
remaining cheese and the breadcrumbs
over the dishes, then season with
pepper. Grill for 5 minutes or until
golden and bubbling. Garnish with
chives and serve with a green salad.

SAVE EFFORT

Keep bags of broccoli and
cauliflower florets in the freezer
ready for this quick fuss-free supper.

Serves 4

Mustard and Caper

Mash 2 hard-boiled egg yolks with
2 tsp smooth Dijon mustard. Add
2 tbsp white wine vinegar and
slowly whisk in 8 tbsp olive oil. Add
2 tbsp chopped capers, 1 tbsp finely
chopped shallot and a pinch of sugar.
Season well with salt and ground
black pepper. Use for grilled fish,
beef, pork or sausages.

Tangy Herb

Put 2 tbsp each freshly chopped
flat-leafed parsley, mint and basil in
a bowl, add 2 tbsp roughly chopped
capers, 1 tsp Dijon mustard, 2 crushed
garlic cloves, 150ml (¼ pint) olive
oil and the juice of ½ lemon and
combine thoroughly using a fork.
Use for grilled or fried steak.

Peanut

Heat 1 tbsp vegetable oil in a pan, add 2 tbsp curry paste, 2 tbsp brown sugar and 2 tbsp peanut butter and fry for 1 minute. Add 200ml (7fl oz) coconut milk and bring to the boil, stirring constantly, then reduce the heat and simmer for 5 minutes. Use for grilled or stir-fried chicken.

Tarragon

Put 500ml (18fl oz) crème fraîche, 1 tsp Dijon mustard and 1 crushed garlic clove in a pan. Bring to the boil, then reduce the heat and simmer for a few minutes. Add 2 tbsp freshly chopped tarragon just before serving. Use for chicken or fish.

Curried Coconut

Heat 2 tbsp extra virgin olive oil in a pan, add 175g (6oz) finely chopped onions with 1 tbsp water and cook gently for 10 minutes or until softened and golden brown. Add 2 crushed garlic cloves, 2.5cm (1in) piece fresh root ginger, peeled and grated, and 3–4 tbsp mild curry paste and cook for 1–2 minutes. Mix 3 tbsp coconut milk powder with 450ml (¾ pint) warm water, stir into the curried mixture and bring to the boil. Let it bubble for 5–10 minutes. Season with salt to taste. Use for fish or shellfish.

Classic Curry

Hands-on time: 5 minutes
Cooking time: about 25 minutes

1 tbsp vegetable oil

1 large onion, finely chopped

1 garlic clove, crushed

4cm (1½in) piece fresh root ginger, peeled and grated

1–2 green chillies, seeded and finely chopped (see Safety Tip, page 76)

¼ tsp ground turmeric

1 tsp each ground coriander and ground cumin

160ml can coconut cream

100ml (3½fl oz) fish stock

500g (1lb 2oz) fresh tomatoes, roughly chopped

400g (14oz) raw king prawns, peeled

salt and freshly ground black pepper

2 tbsp freshly chopped coriander to garnish

boiled basmati rice or naan, lime wedges and chutney to serve

1 Heat the oil in a large pan, add the onion and gently fry for 10 minutes until softened. Add the garlic, ginger, chillies and spices and fry for 2 minutes.

2 Stir in the coconut cream and fish stock, followed by the chopped tomatoes. Season, bring to the boil, then leave to bubble for 5–10 minutes until the sauce has thickened.

3 Add the prawns, reduce the heat and simmer gently for 3 minutes until they turn pink – don't boil or they'll become tough. Check the seasoning and garnish with chopped coriander. Serve with boiled rice or naan, lime wedges and chutney.

Serves 4

Perfect Stir-fry

Stir-fries can be as simple or as substantial as you feel like making them. And if you buy ready-prepared stir-fry vegetables, a meal can be on the table in minutes. Ensure your wok or pan is very hot before you start cooking and keep the ingredients moving.

Stir-frying vegetables

Stir-frying is perfect for non-starchy vegetables, as the quick cooking preserves their colour, freshness and texture.

To serve four, you will need:
450g (1lb) vegetables, 1–2 tbsp vegetable oil, 2 crushed garlic cloves, 2 tbsp soy sauce and 2 tsp sesame oil.

1 Cut the vegetables into even-size pieces. Heat the vegetable oil in a large wok or frying pan until smoking-hot. Add the garlic and cook for a few seconds, then remove and put to one side.
2 Add the vegetables to the wok, and toss and stir them. Keep them moving constantly as they cook, which will take 4–5 minutes.

3 When the vegetables are just tender, but still with a slight bite, turn off the heat. Put the garlic back into the wok and stir well. Add the soy sauce and sesame oil, toss and serve on warmed plates.

2

Stir-frying fish

Choose a firm fish such as monkfish, as more delicate fish will break up.

1 Cut the fish into bite-size pieces. Heat a wok or large pan until very hot and add oil to coat the inside.
2 Add the fish and toss over a high heat for 2 minutes until just cooked. Remove to a bowl.
3 Cook the other ingredients you are using for the stir-fry. Return the fish to the wok or pan for 1 minute to heat through then serve immediately.

Stir-frying poultry and meat

Stir-frying is ideal for poultry and tender cuts of meat.

1 Trim off any fat, then cut the poultry or meat into even-size strips or dice no more than 5mm (¼in) thick. Heat a wok or large pan until hot and add oil to coat the inside.
2 Add the poultry or meat and cook, stirring constantly, until just done. Remove to a bowl. Cook the other ingredients you are using for the stir-fry, then return the poultry or meat to the pan and cook for 1–2 minutes to heat through.

SAVE EFFORT

Cut everything into small pieces of uniform size so that they cook quickly and evenly. If you're cooking onions or garlic with the vegetables, don't keep them over the high heat for too long or they will burn. Add liquids towards the end of cooking so that they don't evaporate.

Sweet and Sour Pork Stir-fry

Hands-on time: 20 minutes
Cooking time: about 10 minutes

2 tbsp vegetable oil

350g (12oz) pork fillet, cut into finger-size pieces

1 red onion, finely sliced

1 red pepper, seeded and finely sliced

2 carrots, cut into thin strips

3 tbsp sweet chilli sauce

1 tbsp white wine vinegar

220g can pineapple slices, roughly chopped, with 2 tbsp juice reserved

a large handful of bean sprouts

½ tbsp sesame seeds

a large handful of fresh coriander, roughly chopped

salt and freshly ground black pepper

boiled long-grain rice to serve

1 Heat the oil over a high heat in a large frying pan or wok. Add the pork, onion, pepper and carrots and cook for 3–5 minutes, stirring frequently, until the meat is cooked through and the vegetables are softening.

2 Stir the sweet chilli sauce, white wine vinegar and reserved pineapple juice into a wok or pan. Bring to the boil, then stir in the pineapple chunks and bean sprouts and heat through. Check the seasoning. Scatter over the sesame seeds and chopped coriander and serve with boiled rice.

Serves 4

Mozzarella and Parma Ham Pizza

Hands-on time: 10 minutes
Cooking time: about 18 minutes

a little plain flour to dust

290g pack pizza base mix

350g (12oz) fresh tomato and chilli
pasta sauce

250g (9oz) buffalo mozzarella, drained
and roughly chopped

6 slices Parma ham, torn into strips

50g (2oz) rocket

a little extra virgin olive oil to drizzle

salt and freshly ground black pepper

SAVE TIME

If you're short of time, buy two
ready-made pizza bases.

1 Preheat the oven to 200°C (180°C
fan oven) mark 6 and lightly flour
two large baking sheets. Mix up the
pizza base according to the pack
instructions. Divide the dough into
two and knead each ball on a lightly
floured surface for about 5 minutes,
then roll them out to make two 23cm
(9in) rounds. Put each on to the
prepared baking sheet.

2 Divide the tomato sauce between the
pizza bases and spread it over, leaving
a small border around each edge.
Scatter over the mozzarella pieces,
then scatter with ham. Season well
with salt and ground black pepper.

3 Cook the pizzas for 15–18 minutes
until golden. Slide on to a wooden
board, top with rocket leaves and
drizzle with olive oil. Cut in half
to serve.

Serves 4

Fish and Chips

Hands-on time: 15 minutes
Cooking time: 12 minutes

4 litres (7 pints) sunflower oil to deep-fry

125g (4oz) self-raising flour

¼ tsp baking powder

¼ tsp salt

1 medium egg

150ml (¼ pint) sparkling mineral water

2 hake fillets, about 125g (4oz) each

450g (1lb) Desirée potatoes, peeled and cut into 1cm (½in) chips

salt, vinegar and Lemon Mayonnaise (see opposite) to serve

1 Heat the oil in a deep-fryer to 190°C (test by frying a small cube of bread; it should brown in 20 seconds).

2 Whiz the flour, baking powder, salt, egg and water in a food processor or blender until combined into a batter. Remove the blade from the food processor. (Alternatively, put the ingredients into a bowl and beat everything together until smooth.) Drop one of the fish fillets into the batter to coat it.

3 Put half the chips into the deep-fryer, then add the battered fish. Fry for 6 minutes or until just cooked, then remove and drain well on kitchen paper. Keep warm if not serving immediately.

4 Drop the remaining fillet into the batter to coat, then repeat step 3 with the remaining chips. Serve with salt, vinegar and Lemon Mayonnaise.

Lemon Mayonnaise

Put 2 medium egg yolks, 2 tsp lemon juice, 1 tsp Dijon mustard and a pinch of sugar into a food processor. Season, then whiz briefly until pale and creamy. With the motor running, slowly pour in 300ml (½ pint) light olive oil through the feeder tube, in a steady stream, until the mayonnaise is thick.

Add 1 tsp grated lemon zest and an additional 1 tbsp lemon juice and whiz briefly to combine. Store the lemon mayonnaise in a screw-topped jar in the fridge. It will keep for up to three days.

Serves 2

Five Main Ingredients

The Well-stocked Fridge and Freezer

The fridge is a vital piece of equipment and keeps food fresh for longer. However, it is the main culprit for waste. The bigger it is, the more it becomes a repository for out-of-date condiments and bags of wilted salad leaves that lurk in its depths.

The fridge
Safe storage
- [ ] Cool cooked food to room temperature before putting in the fridge
- [ ] Wrap or cover all food except fruit and vegetables
- [ ] Practise good fridge discipline: the coldest shelves are at the bottom so store raw meat, fish and poultry there
- [ ] Separate cooked foods from raw foods

To make sure the fridge works properly:
- [ ] Don't overfill it
- [ ] Don't put hot foods in it
- [ ] Don't open the door more than you need to
- [ ] Clean it regularly

The freezer

This is an invaluable storage tool and if you use it properly – particularly with batch cooking – you can save time and avoid wastage. Make sure you allow food time to thaw: if you leave it overnight in the fridge, your meal will be ready to pop into the oven when you get home from work. You can have all sorts of standbys waiting for you: breads, cakes, pastry, frozen vegetables and fruit such as raspberries and blackberries, cream, stocks, soups, herbs and bacon.

How to store food:
- ❑ Freeze food as soon as possible after purchase
- ❑ Label cooked food with the date and name of the dish
- ❑ Freeze food in portions
- ❑ Never put warm foods into the freezer, wait until they have cooled
- ❑ Check the manufacturer's instructions for freezing times
- ❑ Don't refreeze food once it's thawed

What not to store in the freezer:
- ❑ Whole eggs – freeze whites and yolks separately
- ❑ Fried foods – they lose their crispness and can go soggy
- ❑ Some vegetables – cucumber, lettuce and celery have too high a water content
- ❑ Some sauces – mayonnaise and similar sauces will separate when thawed

To make sure the freezer works properly:
- ❑ Defrost it regularly
- ❑ Keep the freezer as full as possible

Thawing and reheating food:
Each recipe will give you instructions on how to reheat the particular dish, but generally:
- ❑ Some foods, such as vegetables, soups and sauces, can be cooked from frozen – dropped into boiling water, or heated gently in a pan until thawed
- ❑ Ensure other foods are thoroughly thawed before cooking
- ❑ Cook food as soon as possible after thawing
- ❑ Ensure the food is piping hot all the way through after cooking

Use Your Microwave to the Max

Having the right equipment can make life so much easier in the kitchen. If you have room for a microwave, it's energy-efficient, quick and easy to use – the busy cook's perfect kitchen companion.

How does it work?

A conventional microwave oven cooks by microwaves that pass through glass, paper, china and plastic and are absorbed by moisture molecules in the food. They penetrate the food to a depth of about 5cm (2in), where they cause the molecules to vibrate and create heat within the food, which cooks it.

The manufacturer's instruction booklet will tell you all you need to know to get the best out of the microwave oven, but here are a few handy tips.

Microwave safety:

❑ The oven will work only if the door is closed

❑ The door has a special seal to prevent microwaves from escaping

❑ Never switch on the microwave when there is nothing inside – the waves will bounce off the walls of the oven and could damage the magnetron (the device that converts electricity into microwaves)

❑ Allow sufficient space around the microwave for ventilation through the air vents

❑ If using plastic containers, use only microwave-proof plastic – ordinary plastic buckles

What to use a microwave for:

- ❑ Cooking ready-prepared meals
- ❑ Cooking vegetables and fish
- ❑ Reheating foods and drinks
- ❑ Softening butter and melting chocolate
- ❑ Drying herbs
- ❑ Scrambling eggs

What not to use a microwave for:

- ❑ Browning meat (unless the oven comes with a browning unit)
- ❑ Soufflés
- ❑ Puff pastry
- ❑ Breaded or battered foods

Microwave tips:

- ❑ Consult the manufacturer's handbook before you use the microwave for the first time
- ❑ Use a plastic trivet so that the microwaves can penetrate the underside of the food
- ❑ Cover fatty foods such as bacon and sausages with kitchen paper to soak up any fat
- ❑ Stir liquids at intervals during microwaving
- ❑ Turn large items of food over during microwaving
- ❑ Clean the interior regularly

Saffron and Red Pepper Risotto

Hands-on time: 20 minutes
Cooking time: about 20 minutes

1 tbsp extra virgin olive oil, plus extra
    to drizzle

300g (11oz) risotto rice

2 large pinches of saffron

150ml (¼ pint) white wine

200g (7oz) roasted red peppers,
    roughly chopped

50g (2oz) rocket

salt and freshly ground black pepper

1 Heat the oil in a large pan over a medium heat. Fry the rice and saffron for 1 minute, then add the white wine and leave to bubble until most of the liquid has been absorbed.

2 Measure 800ml (1¼ pint) of boiling water and add a ladleful to the rice pan and stir until the water has been fully absorbed. Continue this process until the rice is cooked, about 15–18 minutes.

3 Stir through the roasted red peppers and check the seasoning.

4 Serve immediately topped with rocket and a drizzle of extra virgin olive oil.

SAVE MONEY

This recipe shows that you can still create a classic risotto even if you don't happen to have any stock available to hand.

Serves 4

Chicken Laksa

Hands-on time: 10 minutes
Cooking time: about 10 minutes

1 tbsp olive oil

4 × 125g (4oz) chicken breasts, diced

1–3 tbsp green Thai curry paste, to taste

2 sweet potatoes (about 350g/12oz),
  diced

400ml can coconut milk

a large handful of fresh coriander,
  roughly chopped

salt and freshly ground black pepper

1 Heat the oil in a large pan over a
  high heat. Add the chicken breasts,
  Thai curry to taste and the sweet
  potatoes and fry for 5 minutes, stirring
  frequently. Pour in the coconut milk
  and 400ml (14fl oz) hot water.
  Bring to the boil, then reduce the
  heat and simmer for 5 minutes or
  until the chicken and potatoes are
  cooked through.

2 Stir through the coriander and check
  the seasoning. Ladle into warmed
  bowls and serve immediately.

Serves 4

Sticky Drumsticks with Rice and Peas

Hands-on time: 10 minutes
Cooking time: about 25 minutes

8 chicken drumsticks

2 tbsp honey

2 tbsp wholegrain mustard

1 tbsp olive oil

250g (9oz) basmati rice

250g (9oz) frozen peas

salt and freshly ground black pepper

SAVE TIME

Prepare the chicken with the honey, mustard, oil and seasoning up to a day ahead. Cover and chill. Complete the recipe to serve.

1 Preheat the oven to 220°C (200°C fan oven) mark 7. Slash the skin on the drumsticks using a small sharp knife, then put into a roasting tin and mix through the honey, mustard, oil and some seasoning.

2 Roast for 20–25 minutes until the chicken is golden and cooked through. Meanwhile, cook the rice in boiling salted water for 12–15 minutes or until tender, adding the frozen peas for the final 2 minutes of cooking. Drain well.

3 Transfer the chicken to a warmed serving dish. Add 2 tbsp boiling water to the roasting tin and scrape with a wooden spoon to loosen any sticky goodness. Serve the chicken with the rice and peas, and drizzled with the pan juices.

Serves 4

Quick Carbonara

Hands-on time: 10 minutes
Cooking time: about 15 minutes

350g (12oz) dried linguine

½ tbsp olive oil

200g (7oz) unsmoked bacon lardons

4 large eggs, beaten

75g (3oz) freshly grated Parmesan, plus
extra to garnish

salt and freshly ground black pepper

a small handful of fresh parsley,
chopped, to garnish

1 Bring a large pan of water to the boil and cook the linguine according to the pack instructions until it is al dente.

2 Meanwhile, heat the olive oil in a large frying pan and fry the bacon lardons for 5 minutes or until golden. Take the pan off the heat.

3 In a medium bowl, mix together the eggs, grated Parmesan and plenty of ground black pepper.

4 Drain the pasta, keeping 100ml (3½fl oz) of the cooking water to one side. Put the bacon pan back on to a low heat and stir in the pasta water, pasta and egg mixture. Stir for 1 minute until thickened. Check the seasoning, garnish with the parsley and extra Parmesan and serve.

Serves 4

Crusted Cod with Minted Pea Mash

Hands-on time: 10 minutes
Cooking time: about 15 minutes

50g (2oz) sun-dried tomatoes

2 tbsp sun-dried tomato oil (taken from the jar), plus extra to serve

25g (1oz) grated Parmesan

4 skinless cod fillets

500g (1lb 2oz) frozen peas

1 tbsp extra virgin olive oil

a small handful of fresh mint, roughly chopped

salt and freshly ground black pepper

1 Preheat the oven to 200°C (180°C fan oven) mark 6. Put the sun-dried tomatoes, tomato oil from the jar and grated Parmesan into a blender and whiz to make a thick paste. Alternatively, bash the ingredients together using a pestle and mortar.

2 Put the cod on to a non-stick baking sheet and top each piece with a quarter of the tomato mixture. Roast in the oven for 12–15 minutes or until the fish is cooked through and flakes easily when pushed with a knife.

3 Meanwhile, bring a medium pan of water to the boil and cook the peas for 3–4 minutes until tender, then drain. Put the peas into a food processor with the extra virgin olive oil, mint and some seasoning and whiz until the mixture is the consistency of a chunky mash. Serve immediately with the cod and a drizzle of the sun-dried tomato oil.

Serves 4

Ham and Mushroom Turnovers

Hands-on time: 15 minutes
Cooking time: about 30 minutes, plus cooling

1 tbsp extra virgin olive oil

350g (12oz) sliced mushrooms

100g (3½oz) ham, roughly chopped

4 tbsp soft cheese, garlic and
  herb flavour

375g pack ready-rolled puff pastry

salt and freshly ground black pepper

mixed salad leaves and extra virgin
  olive oil to serve

SAVE EFFORT

This versatile recipe is easily
adapted to different filling
combinations – try substituting
grilled artichokes and wilted
spinach or ready-roasted peppers
and goat's cheese.

1 Heat the oil in a large frying pan over
  a medium heat. Fry the mushrooms
  for 5–8 minutes until tender and any
  water in the pan has evaporated.

2 Add the ham and fry for 1 minute. Stir
  in the soft cheese and leave to cool.

3 Preheat the oven to 200°C (180°C fan
  oven) mark 6. Unroll the puff pastry
  and cut into four equal rectangles.

4 Put a quarter of the mushroom
  mixture on one half of each rectangle,
  then brush the pastry edges with
  water. Fold the empty half of the
  pastry over the mushroom mixture
  and press the edges to seal.
  Cut a few slashes into each parcel
  and transfer to a baking tray.

5 Cook for 20 minutes or until puffed
  and golden. Just before serving,
  toss some mixed salad leaves in
  a bowl with a dash of extra virgin
  olive oil and some seasoning. Serve
  immediately with the turnovers.

Serves 4

Beef Fajitas

Hands-on time: 10 minutes
Cooking time: about 10 minutes

1 tbsp olive oil

600g (1lb 5oz) rump or fillet steak, thinly sliced

3 peppers, seeded and finely sliced

1 tbsp Cajun spice

4 flour tortillas

4 tbsp guacamole or soured cream

SAVE MONEY

For a more economical vegetarian version, cut a 227g pack of paneer cheese into finger-size strips, then cook in the oil for 4–5 minutes until golden brown. Put to one side and complete the recipe to serve.

1 Heat the oil in a large frying pan and cook the rump or fillet steak over a medium-high heat for 2–3 minutes for medium-rare meat or longer, if you like.

2 Transfer the steak to a bowl, cover with foil and leave to rest.

3 Add the peppers to the pan with a splash of water and cook for 2–3 minutes until beginning to soften.

4 Put the beef back into the pan, stir in the Cajun spice and heat through. Check the seasoning.

5 Serve the beef mixture in 4 flour tortillas, each topped with 1 tbsp guacamole or soured cream.

Serves 4

Take 5 Quick & Easy Salsas

Quick Tomato

Put 4 roughly chopped tomatoes, ½ ripe, peeled and roughly chopped avocado, 1 tsp olive oil and the juice of ½ lime in a bowl and stir well. Use for grilled fish or chicken.

Smoky

Put 75g (3oz) finely chopped onions or shallots, 150ml (¼ pint) shop-bought barbecue sauce, 100ml (3½fl oz) maple syrup, 1 tbsp cider vinegar, 1 tbsp soft brown sugar, 100ml (3½fl oz) water, 1 tsp lemon juice and a little grated lemon zest in a pan. Bring to the boil and leave to bubble for 10–15 minutes until syrupy. Take the pan off the heat and add 6 finely chopped spring onions and 175g (6oz) finely chopped fresh pineapple. Serve warm or cold. Use for burgers.

Mango and Fennel

Put 1 halved and diced mango, 1 small trimmed and diced fennel bulb, 1 seeded and finely diced chilli, 1 tbsp balsamic vinegar, 2 tbsp freshly chopped flat-leafed parsley and 2 tbsp freshly chopped mint into a bowl. Add the juice of 1 lime, stir to combine and season generously with salt and ground black pepper. Use for grilled chicken.

Avocado, Tomato and Coriander

Put 1 chopped red onion in a bowl and add 1 ripe, peeled and chopped avocado, 4 large roughly chopped tomatoes, a small handful of roughly chopped fresh coriander and the juice of 1 lime. Mix well, then season with salt and ground black pepper. Use at once for grilled pork chops or chicken.

Prawn and Avocado

Put 2 large ripe, peeled and roughly chopped avocados in a large bowl, then add 350g (12oz) cooked, peeled king prawns, 6 small finely sliced spring onions, 3 tbsp freshly chopped coriander, the grated zest and juice of 3 limes and 8 tbsp olive oil. Mix well, then season with salt and ground black pepper. Use for smoked salmon or grilled fish.

Mini Toad in the Holes

Hands-on time: 15 minutes
Cooking time: about 25 minutes

4 tbsp vegetable oil

12 pork sausages

3 large eggs

125g (4oz) plain flour

5 tbsp red onion marmalade

salt and freshly ground black pepper

mixed salad or seasonal vegetables and gravy to serve

1 Preheat the oven to 220°C (200°C fan oven) mark 7. Heat 1 tbsp oil in a large frying pan and fry the pork sausages for 5 minutes or until just turning golden.

2 Divide the remaining 3 tbsp oil equally among the holes of a 12-hole deep muffin tin, then put one browned sausage into each hole. Put the tin into the oven to heat up. Put the frying pan to one side to reuse later.

3 In a large bowl, whisk together the eggs and plain flour to make a thick paste. Gradually whisk in 225ml (8fl oz) water and some seasoning to make a smooth batter. Transfer the mixture to a jug.

4 Remove the tin from the oven and, working quickly, divide the batter among the 12 holes. Put back into the oven and cook for 20 minutes or until the batter is puffed up and golden. Meanwhile, put the frying pan back on to the hob to heat and stir in 5 tbsp water. Bubble for 30 seconds, then add the red onion marmalade and cook for 1 minute to make a thick gravy. Serve immediately with mixed salad or seasonal vegetables.

SAVE EFFORT

Using water in the batter gives crispness and lift to this much-loved comfort food.

Serves 6

Pesto Gnocchi

Hands-on time: 10 minutes
Cooking time: about 5 minutes

2 × 500g bags gnocchi
4 tbsp fresh basil pesto
400g (14oz) mascarpone cheese
1 red chilli, seeded and finely chopped,
  plus extra to garnish (see Safety Tip)
salt and freshly ground black pepper
a large handful of fresh basil,
  roughly chopped, to garnish

1 Bring a large pan of salted water to
  the boil. Add the gnocchi and cook
  according to the pack instructions or
  until the gnocchi bob to the surface
  of the water.
2 Meanwhile, in a medium bowl, mix
  the pesto, mascarpone and chilli with
  some seasoning.
3 Drain the gnocchi and put back
  into the pan. Stir in the mascarpone
  mixture and check the seasoning.
  Serve garnished with chopped chilli
  and basil in warm pasta bowls.

SAFETY TIP

Chillies can be quite mild to
blisteringly hot, depending on the
type of chilli and its ripeness. Taste a
small piece first to check it's not too
hot for you. Be extremely careful when
handling chillies not to touch or rub
your eyes with your fingers, or they will
sting. Wash knives immediately after
handling chillies. As a precaution, use
rubber gloves when preparing them,
if you like.

SAVE EFFORT

The trick with gnocchi is to eat it as
soon as it's ready, or it'll go heavy
and claggy and not be so easy to eat.

Serves 6

All-purpose Lemon Sauce

TAKE
5

Hands-on time: 5 minutes
Cooking time: 4 minutes

grated zest and juice of 2 lemons

175g (6oz) caster sugar

½ tbsp cornflour

50g (2oz) butter

2 medium eggs

sterilised jar

SAVE EFFORT

This versatile sauce is great for scones, cake filling, lemon meringue pie, or simply spreading on crumpets or toast.

1 Whisk together the grated lemon zest and juice, sugar and cornflour in a large, microwave-safe bowl. Add the butter, then microwave on full power (800W) for 2 minutes or until the butter has melted and the mixture is starting to bubble.

2 Crack the eggs into a separate bowl and whisk until thoroughly broken up. Gradually add the eggs to the butter mixture, whisking constantly.

3 Microwave again on full power (800W) for 2 minutes until thickened. Put immediately into a sterilised jar and leave to cool completely, or serve warm spread on toast, crumpets or scones. The potted sauce will keep for up to a week. Once opened, eat within three days.

Makes 375g (13oz)

Easy Peasy
Monthly Meals

Midweek Meal Planner

Week 1

Gruyère and Bacon Frittata

Gammon with Pineapple Salsa

Courgette and Anchovy Burgers

Week 2

Pork Escalopes and Apple Slaw

Orange and Smoked Mackerel Salad

Minted Lamb Puff Pasty

Week 3

Hot-smoked Salmon Salad

Cheat's Oven Kievs

Cauliflower Soup and Blue Cheese Toasties

Week 4

Chicken and Ginger Broth

Herb Lamb Cutlets

Blonde Pizza

Steak with Blue Cheese
Pappardelle

Indian Curried Mussels

Bean and Broccoli Filo
Tart

Roast Curried Chicken

Thai Chicken and
Coconut Rice

Paprika Beef Stew

Mediterranean Sausage
One-pot

Aubergine Bake

Ham and Mustard
Bread and Butter Bake

Barley Risotto

Mexican Beef Bake

Roast Lamb and
Boulangère Potatoes

Meatballs Marinara

Creamy Seafood Lasagne

Barbecue Lamb with
Polenta

Chicken and Preserved
Lemon Tagine

Gruyère and Bacon Frittata

Hands-on time: 10 minutes
Cooking time: about 50 minutes

8 large eggs

75g (3oz) Gruyère, cut into small cubes

a small handful of freshly chopped
  flat-leafed parsley

50g (2oz) watercress, roughly chopped

200g (7oz) bacon lardons

150g (5oz) button mushrooms

175g (6oz) cherry tomatoes

salt and freshly ground black pepper

salad, bread or seasonal vegetables
  to serve

SAVE MONEY

Frittatas are a great way of using
up ends of cooked meats, herbs and
cheese left over in your fridge.

1 Preheat the oven to 200°C (180°C fan oven) mark 6 and line an 18cm × 23cm × 4cm (7in × 9in × 1½in) tin with baking parchment. In a large bowl, beat together the eggs, then stir in the cheese, parsley, half the watercress and a little seasoning. Put to one side.

2 Fry the lardons in a large frying pan over a medium-high heat for 5 minutes or until golden. Lift out and put to one side. Add the mushrooms and tomatoes to the pan and cook for 5 minutes until the mushrooms have softened and the tomatoes are beginning to collapse.

3 Pour the egg mixture into the prepared tin and scatter over the bacon, mushrooms and tomatoes. Cook for 30–40 minutes until golden brown and set. Garnish with the remaining watercress and serve with salad, bread or seasonal vegetables.

Serves 4

Gammon with Pineapple Salsa

Hands-on time: 5 minutes
Cooking time: about 15 minutes

4 × 250g (9oz) gammon steaks

1 tbsp sunflower oil

250g (9oz) fresh pineapple chunks
(or 425g can pineapple chunks in
juice, drained)

1 red chilli, seeded and finely chopped
(see Safety Tip, page 76)

a small handful of fresh mint,
finely chopped

salad to serve

SAVE EFFORT

Add a sprinkling of dried chilli
flakes to the salsa if you don't have
a fresh red chilli to hand.

1 Preheat the grill to high. Line two baking sheets with foil. Snip the fat on each gammon steak at 2cm (¾in) intervals and put 2 steaks on each sheet. Brush the oil over the gammon and grill each tray for 6 minutes, turning the steaks halfway through the cooking time. Cover the cooked gammon with foil to keep warm.

2 Meanwhile, chop the pineapple chunks into smaller pieces. In a medium bowl, stir the pineapple, chilli and mint together until combined. Serve the gammon, drizzled with any juices, with the pineapple salsa and a salad.

Serves 4

Courgette and Anchovy Burgers

Hands-on time: 20 minutes
Cooking time: about 10 minutes

500g (1lb 2oz) courgettes

5 anchovy fillets in oil, finely chopped

50g (2oz) fresh white breadcrumbs

1 medium egg

3 tbsp freshly chopped flat-leafed parsley

1 tbsp wholegrain mustard

plain flour to dust

1 tbsp sunflower oil

4 tbsp natural yogurt

4 tbsp mayonnaise

¼ cucumber, grated

1 tbsp freshly chopped mint

salt and freshly ground black pepper

4 burger buns, toasted (optional) and
salad leaves to serve

1 Trim the courgettes, then grate them coarsely. Wrap the grated courgettes in a clean teatowel and squeeze out as much moisture as you can.

2 Put the courgettes into a large bowl and mix through the chopped anchovies, breadcrumbs, egg, parsley, mustard and some seasoning.

3 Shape the mixture into four patties and dust them in flour. Heat the oil in a large, non-stick frying pan, add the patties and cook for about 8 minutes, carefully turning them once, until golden brown and piping hot.

4 Meanwhile, mix the yogurt, mayonnaise, grated cucumber, mint and some seasoning together in a medium bowl. Serve the patties as they are, or in toasted burger buns, if you like, with the yogurt sauce and some salad leaves.

Serves 4

Steak with Blue Cheese Pappardelle

Hands-on time: 15 minutes
Cooking time: about 15 minutes

350g (12oz) dried pappardelle pasta

1 tbsp sunflower oil

2 × 300g (11oz) rump steaks

250g (9oz) chestnut mushrooms, sliced

200g (7oz) half-fat crème fraîche

40g (1½oz) blue cheese, plus extra
  to garnish

100g (3½oz) bag baby leaf spinach

25g (1oz) walnuts, chopped, to garnish

salt and freshly ground black pepper

1   Bring a large pan of salted water
    to the boil and cook the pasta
    according to the pack instructions.
    Heat half the oil in a large frying
    pan over a high heat. Pat the steaks
    dry with kitchen paper, season well
    and fry for 5–6 minutes for medium
    meat, turning once (cook for shorter/
    longer, if you like). Lift the steaks out
    of the pan and put to one side on a
    board.

2   Carefully wipe the empty pan clean
    with kitchen paper. Put back on to
    the heat and add the remaining oil.
    Fry the mushrooms for 5 minutes
    until softened. Stir in the crème
    fraîche and blue cheese and leave to
    melt. Meanwhile, slice the steaks.

3   Drain the cooked pasta, keeping a
    cupful of the cooking water to one
    side. Put the pasta back into the
    empty pan, then toss through the
    sauce, sliced steak and spinach.
    If needed, add some of the pasta
    cooking water to slacken the
    mixture. Check the seasoning,
    then divide among four plates and
    garnish with walnuts and a little
    extra crumbled blue cheese.
    Serve immediately.

Serves 4

Indian Curried Mussels

Hands-on time: 30 minutes
Cooking time: about 18 minutes

2kg (4½lb) mussels

2 tsp sunflower oil

1 medium onion, finely chopped

4 tbsp mild curry paste

400ml can coconut milk

400ml (13fl oz) vegetable or fish stock

juice of 1 lime

a large handful of fresh coriander, chopped

naan bread to serve (optional)

1 Clean and sort the mussels following the tip below, removing any barnacles and beards with a cutlery knife.

2 Heat the oil in a very large pan with a tight-fitting lid over a medium heat. Fry the onion for 10 minutes until softened, then add the curry paste and fry for 1 minute more. Stir in the coconut milk, stock and lime juice, then turn the heat to high and bring to the boil. Add half the coriander, then tip in the cleaned and sorted mussels.

3 Cover, reduce the heat and simmer for 5-6 minutes, shaking occasionally, or until the mussels have fully opened (discard any that remain closed). Divide among four bowls, scatter over the remaining coriander and serve with naan bread, if you like.

SAVE TIME

Ask your fishmonger for rope-grown mussels, as they are much easier to clean than the dredged variety. They aren't full of silt, either, so can be added directly to soups and stews without making them gritty.

To store fresh mussels safely, keep in an open bag in the fridge, covered lightly with damp kitchen paper (do not submerge in water for prolonged periods of time).

To clean, put in a colander under cold running water. Check to make sure the mussels are alive – the shells should be tightly closed. (Give them a sharp tap on a work surface if they aren't, and discard any that haven't closed after 30 seconds or any that have broken shells.)

Serves 4

Bean and Broccoli Filo Tart

Hand-on time: 20 minutes
Cooking time: about 40 minutes

2 medium eggs

250g (9oz) crème fraîche

150g (5oz) soya beans, frozen

100g (3½oz) broccoli, cut into
small florets

75g (3oz) sunblush tomatoes, chopped

75g (3oz) feta, crumbled

a small handful of fresh mint
leaves, chopped

6 sheets filo pastry (270g pack)

sunflower oil to brush

salt and freshly ground black pepper

green salad to serve

SAVE TIME

Make the tart up to a day ahead.
Cool in tin, cover with foil and chill.
Serve cold or reheat (covered) for
15–20 minutes in an oven preheated
to 180°C (160°C fan oven) mark 4.

1 Preheat the oven to 180°C (160°C fan oven) mark 4. In a large bowl, beat together the eggs, crème fraîche and some seasoning. In a separate bowl, lightly mix together the soya beans, broccoli, tomatoes, feta and mint. Add three-quarters of the mixture to the egg mixture.

2 Brush the top of one of the filo sheets with oil, then lay it in a 20.5cm (8in) round loose-bottomed cake tin, letting the excess hang over the sides. Repeat with remaining sheets, overlapping the sheets slightly each time (there should be no gaps). Pour in the crème fraîche mixture, then scatter over the remaining vegetable mix.

3 Crumple the overhanging pastry down inside the tin (above the level of the filling) and brush the pastry again with oil. Put the tin on a baking sheet and cook for 35–40 minutes or until the filling is set and the pastry is golden. Serve with a salad.

Serves 8

Roast Curried Chicken

Hands-on time: 20 minutes
Cooking time: about 1½ hours

5cm (2in) fresh root ginger

1 whole chicken, about 1.8kg (4lb)

1 lime, halved

40g (1½oz) butter, softened

2 tbsp mild curry paste

800g (1¾lb) new potatoes, halved if large

¾ tbsp plain flour

165ml can coconut milk

1 tsp brown sugar (optional)

salt and freshly ground black pepper

seasonal vegetables to serve

1 Preheat the oven to 190°C (170°C fan oven) mark 5. Roughly chop half the ginger (leave skin on) and put into the cavity of the bird. Add the lime halves and tie the legs together. Put the chicken into a large, sturdy roasting tin. In a small bowl, mix together the butter and half the curry paste. Spread over the top and sides of the bird. Cover with foil and roast for 40 minutes.

2 Carefully remove the foil and add the potatoes to the tin, turning them to coat in the buttery mixture. Put back into the oven and cook for a further 40 minutes or until the potatoes are tender and the chicken is cooked through. Lift the chicken out of the tin and put on a board. Cover loosely with foil and leave to rest. Put the potatoes into a serving dish and keep warm.

3 Spoon off and discard most of the fat in the roasting tin. Put the tin over a medium heat on the hob. Stir in the flour and remaining curry paste, then grate in the remaining ginger. Stirring constantly, add the coconut milk. Fill the empty coconut can with water and add to the pan. Simmer, stirring, for 3–5 minutes until thickened. Check the seasoning and add the sugar, if needed. Serve the chicken, roasted potatoes and gravy with seasonal vegetables.

Serves 4

Week 1 Shopping List

Chilled & Frozen

- ❑ 2 × 300g (11oz) rump steaks
- ❑ 1 whole chicken, about 1.8kg (4lb)
- ❑ 4 × 250g (9oz) gammon steaks
- ❑ 200g (7oz) bacon lardons
- ❑ 2kg (4½lb) mussels
- ❑ 3 medium eggs
- ❑ 8 large eggs
- ❑ 40g (1½oz) butter
- ❑ 200g (7oz) half-fat crème fraîche
- ❑ 250g (9oz) pot crème fraîche
- ❑ about 60g (2½oz) blue cheese
- ❑ 75g (3oz) feta
- ❑ 75g (3oz) Gruyère cheese
- ❑ 4 tbsp natural yogurt
- ❑ 270g pack filo pastry
- ❑ 150g (5oz) frozen soya beans

Fruit, Vegetables & Herbs

- ❑ 1 medium onion
- ❑ 1 red chilli
- ❑ 1 small broccoli
- ❑ 800g (1¾lb) small new potatoes
- ❑ 250g (9oz) pack chestnut mushrooms
- ❑ 150g (5oz) button mushrooms
- ❑ 500g (1lb 2oz) courgettes
- ❑ 175g (6oz) cherry tomatoes
- ❑ ¼ cucumber
- ❑ 250g (9oz) fresh pineapple chunks (or can of pineapple chunks – see Storecupboard)
- ❑ Fresh root ginger
- ❑ 2 limes
- ❑ 50g (2oz) watercress
- ❑ 100g (3½oz) bag baby leaf spinach
- ❑ Pack of fresh mint
- ❑ Pack of fresh coriander
- ❑ Pack of fresh parsley
- ❑ Salad, to serve
- ❑ Seasonal vegetables of your choice, to serve

Storecupboard

(Here's a checklist in case you need
to re-stock)

- ☐ Sunflower oil
- ☐ Vegetable or fish stock
- ☐ Plain flour
- ☐ Brown sugar (optional)
- ☐ 400ml can coconut milk
- ☐ 165ml can coconut milk
- ☐ 350g (12oz) dried pappardelle
  pasta
- ☐ 25g (1oz) walnuts
- ☐ Mild curry paste
- ☐ Wholegrain mustard
- ☐ Mayonnaise
- ☐ Anchovy fillets in oil
- ☐ 75g (3oz) sunblush tomatoes
- ☐ 425g can of pineapple chunks
  (optional)
- ☐ 2 slices white bread
  (for breadcrumbs)
- ☐ Naan bread, to serve (optional)
- ☐ Burger buns, to serve (optional)

Pork Escalopes and Apple Slaw

Hands-on time: 20 minutes
Cooking time: about 5 minutes

200g (7oz) 0% fat Greek yogurt

juice of 1 lemon

1 tsp wholegrain mustard

2 eating apples (skin on), cut into matchsticks

½ small red cabbage, finely shredded

a small handful of fresh parsley, chopped

75g (3oz) Rice Krispies

25g (1oz) plain flour

2 medium eggs, beaten

4 pork escalopes

2 tbsp sunflower oil

salt and freshly ground black pepper

boiled new potatoes to serve

1 Put the yogurt, lemon juice and mustard into a large serving bowl and mix together. Stir in the apple matchsticks, cabbage and parsley. Check the seasoning and put to one side.

2 Whiz the Rice Krispies in a food processor until finely crushed. Tip on to a lipped plate. Put the flour and eggs on two separate lipped plates.

3 Dip each escalope into the flour to coat, tapping off any excess, then dip into the beaten eggs, followed by the cereal crumbs. Finish by dipping each escalope once more into the eggs before coating with a final layer of cereal.

4 Heat the oil in a large non-stick frying pan over a medium heat. Add the escalopes and fry for 5 minutes, turning once, until golden and cooked through. Serve with the apple slaw and boiled new potatoes.

Orange and Smoked Mackerel Salad

🍴 **Hands-on time:** 15 minutes

For the salad

300g (11oz) smoked mackerel, skinned

2 oranges, peeled and pith removed

1 large courgette, cut into ribbons with a peeler

100g bag watercress

40g (1½oz) flaked almonds

crusty bread to serve (optional)

For the dressing

1 tsp wholegrain mustard

1 tsp honey or caster sugar

2 tbsp white wine vinegar

4 tbsp extra virgin olive oil

salt and freshly ground black pepper

1 Flake the mackerel into a large serving bowl. Cut the oranges horizontally (across segments) into slices, then cut each slice in half to make two semi-circles. Discard the pips. Add to the mackerel, together with the courgette ribbons, watercress and most of the almonds.

2 Mix the dressing ingredients together in a small bowl with some seasoning. Drizzle over the salad and toss together lightly. Sprinkle over the remaining almonds and serve with some crusty bread, if you like.

SAVE EFFORT

Make a large batch of the dressing and keep in a sealed jar in the fridge for up to a month, ready to pour over salads whenever you like.

Serves 4

Minted Lamb Puff Pasty

Preparation time: 25 minutes
Cooking time: about 55 minutes, plus cooling

400g pack lamb mince

1 potato, about 175g (6oz), finely diced

1 medium carrot, finely diced

1 small leek, finely sliced

1 garlic clove, finely chopped

few dashes of Worcestershire sauce

2 tbsp tomato purée

½ tbsp dried mint

500g pack puff pastry

plain flour, to dust

1 medium egg, beaten

salad to serve

1 Heat a large frying pan and fry the lamb mince for 5 minutes until cooked through and browned. Lift out of the pan using a slotted spoon and leave to cool. Next, add the potato, carrot, leek and garlic to the pan and cook until just softened, about 10 minutes.

2 Put the lamb back into the pan and add the Worcestershire sauce, tomato purée, mint and a splash of water. Cook for a few minutes, then check the seasoning. Leave to cool completely.

3 Preheat the oven to 200°C (180°C fan oven) mark 6. Cut the pastry into quarters and roll each piece out on a lightly floured worksurface to a rough 18cm (7in) square. Divide the lamb mixture equally among the squares, leaving a 1cm (½in) border of pastry. Brush the pastry with beaten egg, then crimp the edges to seal. Transfer to a baking sheet and brush again with egg. Cook for 30 minutes until deep golden. Serve warm or at room temperature with a salad.

SAVE EFFORT

If you don't have any lamb mince, why not try using beef, chicken or turkey mince instead.

Thai Chicken and Coconut Rice

Hands-on time: 15 minutes
Cooking time: about 30 minutes

1kg (2lb 2oz) mix of chicken thighs
    and drumsticks

1 tbsp sunflower oil

3 tbsp sweet chilli sauce

1 tsp fish sauce

2.5cm (1in) piece fresh root ginger,
    peeled and grated

1 garlic clove, crushed

grated zest and juice of 1 lime

250g (9oz) long-grain rice

4 tbsp desiccated coconut

a small handful of fresh coriander,
    chopped

1. Preheat the oven to 200°C (180°C fan oven) mark 6. Put the chicken pieces into a roasting tin just large enough to hold them in a single layer. Add the oil, chilli sauce, fish sauce, ginger, garlic, lime zest and juice. Stir together (using your hands is easiest). Turn the chicken pieces, skin side up, and cook for 30 minutes or until cooked through.

2. When the chicken has 15 minutes left in the oven, cook the rice according to the pack instructions, adding the desiccated coconut after 5 minutes.

3. Stir the coriander through the finished cooked rice and serve with the chicken, drizzled with pan juices.

SAVE TIME

Put the chicken and marinade ingredients into a large sandwich bag and massage well. Chill for up to a day. Tip mixture into a roasting tin and complete the recipe to serve.

Paprika Beef Stew

Hands-on time: 20 minutes
Cooking time: 1¼ hours

1 tbsp sunflower oil

750g (1lb 11oz) braising steak, excess fat trimmed, cut into 2cm (¾in) cubes

25g (1oz) plain flour

1 red onion, roughly chopped

1 each red and green pepper, seeded and roughly chopped

1½ tsp paprika

5 tbsp tomato purée

500ml (17fl oz) beef stock

250g (9oz) long-grain rice

fresh coriander or parsley to garnish

cream, to drizzle (optional)

1 Heat the oil in a large pan over a medium heat. Meanwhile, dust the beef with the flour, making sure every bit is coated. Brown the beef in the pan (do this in batches if necessary to avoid overcrowding the pan).

2 Once all the beef is browned and put back into the pan, add the onion, peppers, paprika and tomato purée and fry for 5 minutes. Pour in the stock, bring to the boil, then cover, reduce the heat and simmer for 1 hour or until the beef is tender. Take the lid off for the final 15 minutes of the cooking time, stirring occasionally.

3 When the beef has 15 minutes left to cook, boil the rice according to the pack instructions.

4 Check the stew seasoning. Garnish the beef with the coriander or parsley and a drizzle of cream, if you like. Serve with the rice.

FREEZE AHEAD

Prepare to the end of step 2, leave to cool completely, then cover and freeze for up to a month. To serve, defrost thoroughly, gently reheat and complete the recipe.

Serves 4

Mediterranean Sausage One-pot

Hands-on time: 15 minutes
Cooking time: 40 minutes

8 pork sausages

1 red onion, cut into 8 wedges

1 tbsp fresh oregano, roughly chopped (or use ½ tbsp dried oregano), plus extra to garnish

5 garlic cloves, skin on

3 medium sweet potatoes, about 500g (1lb 2oz), cut into 2.5cm (1in) chunks

2 tbsp extra virgin olive oil

3 tomatoes, cut into wedges

50g (2oz) black olives, pitted

salt and freshly ground black pepper

crusty bread to serve (optional)

1 Preheat the oven to 200°C (180°C fan oven) mark 6. Put the sausages into a large roasting tin and add the onion wedges, oregano, garlic, sweet potatoes, oil and plenty of seasoning. Toss everything together, then roast for 30 minutes.

2 Add the tomato wedges and black olives and put back into the oven for 10 minutes. Garnish with extra oregano and, if you like, serve with some crusty bread.

SAVE EFFORT

Buy the best-quality sausages, so they brown nicely and don't split and burst.

Serves 4

Aubergine Bake

Hands-on time: 30 minutes
Cooking time: about 45 minutes

2 aubergines, cut lengthways into
   1cm (½in) wide strips

2½ tbsp extra virgin olive oil

1 onion, finely chopped

2 garlic cloves, crushed

2 × 400g cans chopped tomatoes

½ tbsp dried oregano

a large pinch of caster sugar

a large handful of fresh basil, chopped

2 × 125g mozzarella balls, torn
   into pieces

25g (1oz) Parmesan cheese, grated

salt

crusty bread and a crisp salad to serve

1 Preheat the grill to medium. Arrange
the aubergine slices on two large
baking sheets. Brush with half the
oil. Sprinkle over a little salt and grill
each tray separately for 12 minutes,
turning the slices halfway through.
Put to one side.

2 Meanwhile, heat the remaining oil in a
large pan over a medium heat and fry
the onion for 10 minutes until soft. Add
the garlic and fry for 1 minute more,
then add the tomatoes, oregano and
sugar. Bring to the boil, reduce the heat
and simmer for 15 minutes until thick
and pulpy. Stir in most of the basil.

3 Preheat the oven to 220°C (200°C
fan oven) mark 7. Spoon a thin layer
of the sauce into a 1.8 litre (3¼ pint)
heatproof serving dish, then dot over
a third of the mozarella. Cover with
a layer of grilled aubergine, then
repeat the layering process twice
more, finishing with a layer of sauce
and mozzarella.

4 Sprinkle over the Parmesan cheese
and cook for 15–20 minutes until
bubbling and golden. Garnish with
the remaining basil and serve with
crusty bread and a crisp green salad.

SAVE TIME

Prepare to the end of step 3 up to
a day ahead. Cool, cover and chill.
Complete the recipe to serve; allow
an extra 5 minutes cooking time.

Serves 4

Week 2 Shopping List

Chilled & Frozen

- [ ] 750g (1lb 11oz) braising steak
- [ ] 400g pack lamb mince
- [ ] 1kg (2lb 2oz) mix of chicken thighs and drumsticks
- [ ] 4 pork escalopes
- [ ] 8 good-quality pork sausages
- [ ] 300g (11oz) smoked mackerel
- [ ] 3 medium eggs
- [ ] 200g (7oz) 0% fat Greek yogurt
- [ ] Cream (optional)
- [ ] 2 × 125g mozzarella balls
- [ ] 25g (1oz) Parmesan cheese
- [ ] 500g pack puff pastry

Fruit, Vegetables & Herbs

- [ ] 1 onion
- [ ] 2 red onions
- [ ] 1 small leek
- [ ] 2 garlic bulbs
- [ ] 1 red pepper
- [ ] 1 green pepper
- [ ] 2 aubergines
- [ ] 1 medium carrot
- [ ] 1 potato, about 175g (6oz)
- [ ] 3 medium sweet potatoes
- [ ] New potatoes, to serve
- [ ] 3 tomatoes
- [ ] 1 large courgette
- [ ] Fresh root ginger
- [ ] 1 small red cabbage
- [ ] 1 lemon
- [ ] 2 oranges
- [ ] 1 lime
- [ ] 2 eating apples
- [ ] 100g bag watercress
- [ ] Pack of fresh parsley
- [ ] Pack of fresh coriander
- [ ] Pack of fresh oregano (or dried)
- [ ] Pack of fresh basil
- [ ] Salad, to serve

Storecupboard

(Here's a checklist in case you
need to re-stock)

- ❏ Sunflower oil
- ❏ Extra virgin olive oil
- ❏ Beef stock
- ❏ Plain flour
- ❏ Paprika
- ❏ Wholegrain mustard
- ❏ White wine vinegar
- ❏ Worcestershire sauce
- ❏ Fish sauce
- ❏ Sweet chilli sauce
- ❏ Honey or sugar
- ❏ Caster sugar
- ❏ 2 × 400g cans chopped tomatoes
- ❏ 7 tbsp tomato purée
- ❏ 40g (1½oz) flaked almonds
- ❏ Desiccated coconut
- ❏ Dried mint
- ❏ Dried oregano
- ❏ 50g (2oz) black olives
- ❏ 75g (3oz) Rice Krispies
- ❏ 500g (1lb 2oz) long-grain rice
- ❏ Crusty bread, to serve (optional)

Hot-smoked Salmon Salad

Hands-on time: 15 minutes
Cooking time: 8 minutes

4 medium eggs

300g (11oz) small new potatoes, quartered

200g (7oz) fine green beans, trimmed and halved

100g (3½oz) radishes, thinly sliced

80g bag salad leaves

50g (2oz) ready-made croûtons

250g (9oz) hot-smoked salmon, skinned and flaked

lemon wedges to serve

For the dressing

3 tbsp sweet chilli sauce

1 tbsp freshly chopped chives

2 tbsp extra virgin olive oil

salt and freshly ground black pepper

SAVE TIME

Boil and drain the eggs, potatoes and beans, then chill until needed.

1 Bring two small pans of water to the boil. To one, add the eggs, reduce the heat and simmer for 7 minutes. To the other, add the potatoes and beans and cook for 6 minutes until tender.

2 Meanwhile, put the radishes into a large bowl with the salad leaves, croûtons and salmon flakes. In a small bowl, mix together the dressing ingredients with some seasoning.

3 Drain the potatoes and beans and leave to steam-dry in a colander. Lift out the eggs and run under cold water then shell and quarter. Add the potatoes and beans to the salad bowl and toss gently. Divide the salad mixture among four plates and top each with a quartered egg. Drizzle over the dressing and serve with lemon wedges.

Serves 4

Cheat's Oven Kievs

Hands-on time: 15 minutes
Cooking time: 25 minutes

4 × 125g (4oz) skinless chicken breasts

50g (2oz) garlic and herb soft cheese

4 cocktail sticks

75g (3oz) fresh white breadcrumbs

1 medium egg

25g (1oz) butter, melted

a small handful of fresh curly parsley, finely chopped

salt and freshly ground black pepper

green salad and boiled new potatoes to serve

1 Preheat the oven to 200°C (180°C fan oven) mark 6. Cut a slit in the side of a chicken breast and use your finger to work it into a pocket. Repeat with the remaining breasts. Stuff each pocket with a quarter of the soft cheese, seal with a cocktail stick and arrange the breasts on a non-stick baking sheet.

2 In a medium bowl, mix together the remaining ingredients and some seasoning. Pat a quarter of the bread mixture on top of each chicken breast.

3 Cook for 25 minutes or until the breasts are cooked through. Remove the cocktail sticks and serve with a green salad and boiled new potatoes.

FREEZE AHEAD

Complete the recipe to the end of step 2. Leaving the chicken on the sheet, wrap well in clingfilm and freeze for up to a month. To serve, allow the chicken to defrost on the sheet in the fridge overnight, then unwrap the clingfilm and complete the recipe.

Serves 4

Cauliflower Soup and Blue Cheese Toasties

Hands-on time: 20 minutes
Cooking time: about 30 minutes

1 tbsp sunflower oil

1kg (2lb 2oz) cauliflower, leaves trimmed, cut into small florets

2 medium potatoes, about 450g (1lb), chopped

½ tsp Dijon mustard

1.1 litres (2 pints) vegetable or chicken stock

200ml (7fl oz) semi-skimmed milk

8 small slices sourdough bread

100g (3½oz) blue cheese, crumbled

½–1 red chilli, seeded and finely chopped (see Safety Tip, page 76)

1 tbsp chopped fresh chives

1 Heat the oil in a large pan over a medium heat and fry the cauliflower and potatoes for 8–10 minutes until starting to soften. Stir in the mustard, then pour in the stock and milk and bring to the boil. Reduce the heat and simmer for 15 minutes until the vegetables are tender, then whiz in a blender until smooth (do this in batches if necessary). Pour back into the pan and check the seasoning.

2 Preheat the grill to medium. Arrange the bread slices on a baking sheet and toast on one side until golden. Scatter the cheese and chilli over the untoasted side, then grill for 3–5 minutes until the cheese is bubbling and golden. Reheat the soup if necessary and divide among four warmed soup bowls. Season with ground black pepper, scatter over the chives and serve with the toasts.

FREEZE AHEAD

Make extra batches of cauliflower soup and freeze individual servings ready for a quick lunch or light supper.

Serves 4

Ham and Mustard Bread and Butter Bake

🍴 **Hands-on time:** 15 minutes, plus optional soaking
Cooking time: about 35 minutes

10 medium slices white bread

40g (1½oz) butter, softened

1 tbsp wholegrain mustard

150g (5oz) ham slices

275ml (9fl oz) whole milk

275ml (9fl oz) double cream

4 medium eggs

50g (2oz) mature Cheddar, grated

salt and freshly ground black pepper

crisp green salad to serve

SAVE EFFORT

If you don't have any ham, this recipe also works well with chicken or beef.

1 Lay five of the bread slices on a board. Spread over the butter and mustard. Next, divide the ham among the bread slices and finish by laying another piece of bread on top of each stack. Cut the sandwiches into quarters on the diagonal.

2 Arrange the triangles in a not-too-deep 23cm × 23cm × 7.5cm (9in × 9in × 3in) ovenproof serving dish. In a large jug, mix together the milk, cream, eggs and plenty of seasoning until well combined. Pour the egg mixture evenly over the bread, then press the bread down a little. Leave to soak in the fridge for 15 minutes, if you have time, otherwise carry straight on.

3 Preheat the oven to 180°C (160°C fan oven) mark 4. Scatter over the cheese and season with ground black pepper. Cook for 30–35 minutes until the egg mixture has set. Serve immediately with a crisp green salad.

Serves 4–6

Barley Risotto

Hands-on time: 10 minutes
Cooking time: about 50 minutes

1 tbsp extra virgin olive oil

1 large onion, finely chopped

300g (11oz) pearl barley

50ml (2fl oz) white wine

1.3 litres (2¼ pints) hot vegetable stock

1 tbsp tapenade

½ small head broccoli, cut into
  small florets

200g (7oz) frozen peas

a small handful of rocket

salt and freshly ground black pepper

grated Parmesan to serve (optional)

1 Heat the oil in a large pan over
a medium heat. Fry the onion for
10 minutes until soft. Stir in the barley
and fry for 1 minute, then pour in the
wine, bring to the boil, reduce the heat
and simmer, stirring, for 2 minutes.

2 Gradually add the hot stock, stirring
well after each addition. Only add
the next ladleful of stock once the
previous one has been absorbed.
Continue until the barley is cooked –
about 30 minutes – but you don't need
to stir all the time and might not need
all the stock.

3 Stir through the tapenade, then add
the broccoli and peas and cook for
3 minutes more. Season, then stir
through the rocket and serve topped
with grated cheese, if you like.

Serves 4

Mexican Beef Bake

Hands-on time: 15 minutes
Cooking time: about 30 minutes

1 tbsp sunflower oil

1 large onion, finely chopped

500g pack beef mince

1–2 green chillies, seeded and finely chopped (see Safety Tip, page 76)

400g can chopped tomatoes

410g can kidney beans, drained and rinsed

a large handful of fresh coriander, roughly chopped

100g (3½oz) tortilla chips (lightly salted)

50g (2oz) mature Cheddar, grated

soured cream and a crisp green salad to serve

1 Heat the oil in a large pan and gently cook the onion until softened, about 10 minutes. Turn up the heat and stir in the beef and cook until all the meat is well browned, about 10 minutes.

2 Add the chillies, tomatoes, kidney beans and plenty of seasoning and cook for 5 minutes. Stir in the coriander and check the seasoning. Empty the mixture into a heatproof serving dish.

3 Preheat the grill to medium. Top the beef mixture with the tortilla chips and cheese. Grill until piping hot and the cheese is melted and golden. Serve immediately with some soured cream and a crisp green salad.

SAVE TIME

Prepare to the end of step 2, cover and store in the fridge until needed. To serve, reheat the chilli beef then continue with step 3.

Serves 4

Roast Lamb and Boulangère Potatoes

Hands-on time: 25 minutes
Cooking time: about 1½ hours

2kg (4½lb) Maris Piper potatoes, thinly sliced into rounds – a mandolin is ideal for this

1 large onion, thinly sliced

10 thyme sprigs

400ml (13fl oz) hot chicken stock

2 camomile teabags

2 tsp sunflower oil

1.6kg (3½lb) lamb shoulder

salt and freshly ground black pepper

mint sauce or redcurrant jelly and seasonal vegetables to serve

1 Preheat the oven to 200°C (180°C fan oven) mark 6. Layer the potato slices, onion and half of the thyme in a 2.5 litre (4½ pint) heatproof serving dish, seasoning as you go. Pour over the stock. Put a large wire rack over the dish.

2 Empty the contents of the camomile teabags into a small bowl (discard the bags). Stir in the leaves from the remaining thyme, some seasoning and the oil. Rub the camomile mixture over the lamb. Sit the lamb on the wire rack on top of the dish. Cover everything with foil.

3 Carefully transfer the dish to the oven and roast for 1 hour. Uncover and cook for 30 minutes more (the lamb should be cooked to medium) or until the lamb is cooked to your liking, and the potatoes are tender and golden.

4 Transfer the lamb to a board, cover with foil and leave to rest for 20 minutes; keep the potatoes warm in the oven. Serve the lamb and potatoes with mint sauce or redcurrant jelly and seasonal vegetables.

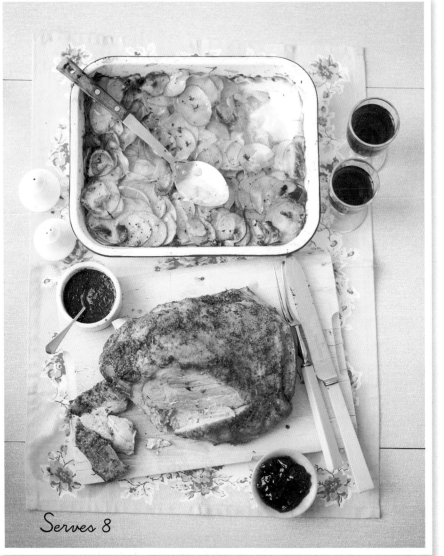

Serves 8

Week 3 Shopping List

Chilled & Frozen

- [ ] 500g pack beef mince
- [ ] 1.6kg (3½lb) lamb shoulder
- [ ] 4 × 125g (4oz) skinless chicken breasts
- [ ] 250g (9oz) hot-smoked salmon
- [ ] 150g (5oz) ham slices
- [ ] 9 medium eggs
- [ ] 65g (2½oz) butter
- [ ] 275ml (9fl oz) double cream
- [ ] Soured cream, to serve
- [ ] 50g (2oz) soft cheese, garlic and herb flavour
- [ ] 100g (3½oz) blue cheese
- [ ] 100g (3½oz) mature Cheddar cheese
- [ ] Parmesan cheese (optional)
- [ ] 275ml (9fl oz) whole milk
- [ ] 200ml (7fl oz) semi-skimmed milk
- [ ] 200g (7oz) frozen peas

Fruit, Vegetables & Herbs

- [ ] 3 large onions
- [ ] 100g (3½oz) radishes
- [ ] 1 red chilli
- [ ] 1–2 green chillies
- [ ] 200g (7oz) fine green beans
- [ ] ½ small head broccoli
- [ ] 1kg (2lb 2oz) cauliflower
- [ ] 300g (11oz) small new potatoes
- [ ] New potatoes, to serve
- [ ] 2.5kg (5½lb) Maris Piper potatoes
- [ ] Seasonal vegetables, to serve
- [ ] 1 lemon
- [ ] Pack of fresh chives
- [ ] Pack of curly parsley
- [ ] Pack of fresh coriander
- [ ] Pack of fresh thyme
- [ ] Small handful of rocket
- [ ] 80g bag salad leaves
- [ ] 3 × salads, to serve

Storecupboard

(Here's a checklist in case you need to re-stock)

- ☐ Sunflower oil
- ☐ Extra virgin olive oil
- ☐ Vegetable stock
- ☐ Chicken stock
- ☐ White wine
- ☐ 400g can chopped tomatoes
- ☐ 410g can kidney beans
- ☐ Wholegrain mustard
- ☐ Dijon mustard
- ☐ Sweet chilli sauce
- ☐ Mint sauce (optional)
- ☐ Redcurrant jelly (optional)
- ☐ Tapenade
- ☐ 300g (11oz) pearl barley
- ☐ 50g (2oz) ready-made croûtons
- ☐ 1 large loaf sliced white bread
- ☐ Sourdough bread
- ☐ 100g (3½oz) tortilla chips, lightly salted
- ☐ 2 camomile teabags
- ☐ 4 cocktail sticks

Chicken and Ginger Broth

Hands-on time: 15 minutes
Cooking time: about 10 minutes

3 × 125g (4oz) skinless chicken breasts, cut into strips

1.4 litres (2½ pints) strong chicken stock

4cm (1½in) piece fresh root ginger, peeled and cut into matchsticks

½–1 red chilli, seeded and finely sliced (see Safety Tip, page 76)

125g pack baby sweetcorn, roughly chopped

2 large carrots, cut into matchsticks

200g (7oz) uncooked egg noodles or 250g (8oz) boiled rice

4 spring onions, finely sliced

a small handful of fresh parsley, finely chopped, to garnish

SAVE MONEY

If you have any leftover roast chicken, use this instead of poaching the chicken specially for this soup. Simply add to the simmering stock to warm through for a quick and economical supper.

1 Put the chicken breasts into a medium pan and cover with cold water. Bring to the boil, reduce the heat and simmer gently for 5 minutes or until cooked through.

2 Meanwhile, in a large pan, bring the stock to the boil and add the ginger and chilli. Reduce the heat and simmer for a few minutes, then add the sweetcorn, carrots, noodles or rice and most of the spring onions. Simmer for 3 minutes until the noodles are cooked and the vegetables are just softening.

3 Drain the cooked chicken and divide the broth among four soup bowls. Ladle over the stock mixture, sprinkle over the remaining spring onions and the parsley and serve.

Serves 4

Herb Lamb Cutlets

Hands-on time: 10 minutes
Cooking time: about 14 minutes

12 lamb cutlets

1½ tbsp Dijon mustard

a large handful of fresh parsley, chopped

a large handful of fresh mint, chopped

salt and freshly ground black pepper

boiled new potatoes and a salad to serve

1 Preheat the grill to medium-high. Brush the lamb cutlets with mustard and sprinkle over a little seasoning.

2 Mix the parsley and mint together in a small bowl, then tip on to a plate. Dip each side of the lamb cutlets in the herbs, then put on to a non-stick baking sheet.

3 Grill the lamb for 10–14 minutes (depending on the thickness and how you like your meat cooked), turning once. Serve with boiled new potatoes and a salad.

SAVE MONEY

Use any combination of chopped fresh herbs you have to hand – coriander, chives and rosemary all work well.

Serves 4

Blonde Pizza

Hands-on time: 20 minutes, plus rising
Cooking time: 25 minutes

300g (11oz) strong white bread flour,
    plus extra to dust

1 tsp fast-action dried yeast

1 tsp caster sugar

½ tsp extra virgin olive oil, plus extra
    to drizzle

1 small courgette, cut into ribbons with
    a peeler

½ red onion, finely sliced

125g (4oz) mozzarella ball, torn
    into pieces

1 red chilli, seeded and finely sliced (see
    Safety Tip, page 76)

salt and freshly ground black pepper

a small handful of rocket to garnish

1 Put the flour, yeast, sugar and ½ tsp salt
   into a large bowl. Quickly mix in 250ml
   (9fl oz) warm water to make a soft,
   but not sticky dough (add more flour/
   water as needed). Knead on a floured
   worksurface for 5 minutes. Form into a
   ball, cover with a teatowel and leave for
   15 minutes.

2 Preheat the oven to 220°C (200°C fan
   oven) mark 7 and put a large non-stick
   baking sheet in to heat up. Roll out
   the dough to a thin circle about 38cm
   (15in) in diameter – keep dusting
   the surface with flour as needed.
   Carefully transfer the pizza base to
   the preheated baking sheet and brush
   the base with oil. Cook for 10 minutes.

3 Take the sheet out of the oven and
   scatter the courgette, red onion,
   mozzarella and chilli over the base.
   Put back into the oven for 15 minutes.
   Season and garnish with rocket,
   drizzle over the extra oil and serve
   immediately.

FREEZE AHEAD

Prepare to the end of step 1, but
don't leave to rise. Transfer to an
oiled freezer bag and freeze for up
to a month. Defrost and complete
the recipe to serve.

Serves 4

Meatballs Marinara

Hands-on time: 15 minutes
Cooking time: about 35 minutes

500g pack beef mince

¼ tsp ground cinnamon

1 onion, finely chopped

1½ tbsp oil

2 × 400g cans chopped tomatoes

a large pinch of sugar

1 tsp dried thyme

a small handful of fresh basil, chopped

salt and freshly ground black pepper

boiled rice to serve

1 In a food processor, whiz the mince, cinnamon, half the chopped onion and plenty of seasoning. Form the mixture into 16 rounds, each about the size of a golf ball.

2 Heat the oil in a large frying pan over a medium-high heat and brown the meatballs until golden all over (about 8 minutes). Remove the meatballs from the pan and put to one side. Fry the the remaining onion for 8 minutes over a medium heat until softened, then stir in the tomatoes, sugar and thyme.

3 Put the meatballs back into the pan, then bring to the boil. Reduce the heat and simmer for 15 minutes until the sauce has thickened slightly and the meatballs are cooked through.

4 Check the seasoning, scatter over the basil and serve immediately with boiled rice.

FREEZE AHEAD

Prepare to the end of step 2. Cool completely, then transfer to a freezerproof container. Cover and freeze for up to a month. To serve, defrost overnight in the fridge, then empty the meatballs into a pan and reheat gently. Complete the recipe to serve.

Serves 4

Creamy Seafood Lasagne

Hands-on time: 15 minutes
Cooking time: about 25 minutes

1 tbsp sunflower oil

2 × 320g packs fish-pie mix

200g (7oz) raw peeled prawns

6 dried lasagne sheets, each measuring 16cm × 8cm (6½in × 3½in)

400g (14oz) mascarpone cheese

2 tbsp freshly chopped dill

125g (4oz) ciabatta, chopped into rough pieces

salt and freshly ground black pepper

crisp green salad to serve

1 Preheat the oven to 180°C (160°C fan oven) mark 4. Heat half the oil in a large frying pan over a high heat and fry the fish and prawns for 2 minutes until beginning to turn opaque. Tip into a sieve and allow any excess liquid to drain off.

2 Meanwhile, put the lasagne sheets into a heatproof dish and cover with boiling water. Leave to soak for 3–5 minutes until beginning to soften. In a large bowl, stir together the mascarpone, most of the dill and plenty of seasoning. Carefully fold in the fish and prawns, trying not to break up the fish too much.

3 Spoon a third of the fish mixture into a 1.8 litre (3¼ pint) serving dish, then cover with a layer of lasagne sheets (you may need to tear one in half). Continue to layer until you've used up all the fish mixture and lasagne sheets, finishing with a layer of fish.

4 In a medium bowl, stir together the ciabatta pieces and the remaining dill and sunflower oil. Sprinkle the bread mixture on top of the fish mixture. Cook for 15–20 minutes until the lasagne is bubbling and the crumb topping is golden. Serve immediately with a crisp green salad.

Serves 6

Barbecue Lamb with Polenta

Hands-on time: 20 minutes
Cooking time: about 1¼ hours

For the lamb

½ tbsp olive oil

400g (14oz) lamb shoulder, diced

1 large onion, finely sliced

1-2 red chillies, seeded and finely chopped (see Safety Tip, page 76)

400g can chopped tomatoes

2 tbsp soy sauce

2 tbsp dark brown sugar

5 tbsp tomato ketchup

300ml (½ pint) lamb or chicken stock

salt and freshly ground black pepper

For the polenta

1.5 litres (2½ pints) chicken stock

375g (13oz) quick-cook polenta

a large handful of fresh coriander, roughly chopped

1 Heat the oil in a large pan and brown the lamb (in batches if necessary). Add the onion to the pan and cook gently for 10 minutes.

2 Stir in the chillies, tomatoes, soy, sugar, ketchup, stock and seasoning. Bring to the boil, cover, reduce the heat and simmer for 1 hour until the lamb is tender. Check seasoning.

3 About 10 minutes before the lamb is ready, make the polenta. Pour the chicken stock into a large pan and bring to the boil. When bubbling, quickly whisk in the polenta and stir to thicken (you might need more stock/water, as it thickens quickly). Stir in the coriander and check the seasoning (it will need plenty!). Serve with the lamb.

SAVE TIME

Prepare to the end of step 2 up to two days ahead. Chill until needed.

Serves 4

Chicken and Preserved Lemon Tagine

🍴 **Hands-on time:** 20 minutes
Cooking time: about 1 hour 5 minutes

---

1 tbsp olive oil

8 chicken thighs, about 800g (1lb 12oz)

1 large onion, finely sliced

1 tsp each ground ginger, cinnamon
and cumin

a large pinch of saffron

500ml (18fl oz) chicken stock

3 small preserved lemons, seeded
and chopped

40g (1½oz) green olives, pitted and
roughly chopped

200g (7oz) couscous

salt and freshly ground black pepper

a large handful of fresh coriander,
chopped, to garnish

1 In a large, heavy-based pan, heat the oil over a high heat and brown the chicken pieces (do this in batches if necessary to avoid overcrowding the pan). Lift out and put to one side.

2 Turn the heat to medium and add the onion. Cook until softened, about 10 minutes. Add the spices and cook for 1 minute. Put the chicken and any juices back into the pan and pour over the stock. Bring to the boil, cover, reduce the heat and simmer for 30 minutes.

3 Uncover, stir in the chopped preserved lemons and olives and simmer uncovered for 15 minutes.

4 Meanwhile, put the couscous in a bowl and pour over boiling water until just covered. Cover with clingfilm and leave for 10 minutes. Fluff up the couscous with a fork and check the seasoning of the tagine. Garnish with chopped coriander and serve with the couscous.

Serves 4

Week 4 Shopping List

Chilled & Frozen

- [ ] 500g pack beef mince
- [ ] 400g (14oz) diced lamb shoulder
- [ ] 12 lamb cutlets
- [ ] 3 × 125g (4oz) skinless chicken breasts
- [ ] 8 chicken thighs, about 800g (1¾lb)
- [ ] 2 × 320g packs fish-pie mix
- [ ] 200g (7oz) raw peeled prawns
- [ ] 400g (14oz) mascarpone cheese
- [ ] 125g (4oz) mozzarella ball

Fruit, Vegetables & Herbs

- [ ] 1 onion
- [ ] 2 large onions
- [ ] 1 red onion
- [ ] 4 spring onions
- [ ] 4 red chillies
- [ ] 1 small courgette
- [ ] 2 large carrots
- [ ] 125g pack baby sweetcorn
- [ ] New potatoes, to serve
- [ ] Fresh root ginger
- [ ] Large pack of fresh parsley
- [ ] Pack of fresh mint
- [ ] Pack of fresh basil
- [ ] Pack of fresh coriander
- [ ] Pack of fresh dill
- [ ] Small bag of rocket
- [ ] 2 × salads, to serve

Storecupboard
(Here's a checklist in case you need to re-stock)

- ❏ Sunflower oil
- ❏ Extra virgin olive oil
- ❏ Olive oil
- ❏ Chicken stock
- ❏ Lamb stock (optional)
- ❏ Strong white bread flour
- ❏ Caster sugar
- ❏ Dark brown sugar
- ❏ Fast-action dried yeast
- ❏ 3 × 400g cans chopped tomatoes
- ❏ Tomato ketchup
- ❏ Dijon mustard
- ❏ Soy sauce
- ❏ Dried thyme

- ❏ Ground cinnamon
- ❏ Ground ginger
- ❏ Ground cumin
- ❏ Saffron threads
- ❏ 375g (13oz) quick-cook polenta
- ❏ 200g (7oz) couscous
- ❏ 6 dried lasagne sheets, each measuring 16cm × 8cm (6½in × 3½in)
- ❏ 200g (7oz) egg noodles
- ❏ Long-grain rice, to serve
- ❏ 3 small preserved lemons
- ❏ 40g (1½oz) green olives
- ❏ 125g (4oz) ciabatta bread

Easy Peasy Puds

Marbled Mousse

Hands-on time: 25 minutes, plus chilling
Cooking time: 10 minutes, plus cooling

125g (4oz) good-quality plain chocolate, finely chopped, plus extra shavings to decorate

125g (4oz) good-quality white chocolate, finely chopped

4 large eggs

75g (3oz) caster sugar

400ml (13½fl oz) double cream

1 Melt 100g (3½oz) of the plain chocolate in a heatproof bowl over a pan of gently simmering water, making sure the bowl doesn't touch the water. Take off the heat and leave to cool for 15 minutes. Meanwhile, using the same method, melt 100g (3½oz) of the white chocolate.

2 Separate the eggs and put the yolks into one large bowl and the whites in another. Using electric beaters, whisk the yolks with the sugar until pale and moussey – about 5 minutes. In another bowl, using the same beaters, whip the cream until just holding its shape. Wash and dry the beaters, then whisk the egg whites until stiff but not dry.

3 Using a large metal spoon, fold the cream into the yolk and sugar mixture, followed by the egg whites. Spoon half the mixture into one of the now-empty bowls. Fold the cooled and melted plain chocolate and remaining chopped white chocolate into one bowl of mixture, then stir the melted and cooled white chocolate and remaining chopped plain chocolate into the other.

4 Spoon one mousse on top of the other and lightly fold the two together to get a marbled effect. Divide the mixture among six glasses. Cover and chill for 4 hours or overnight. Top with chocolate shavings before serving.

Note: As this pudding contains raw eggs, buy those with the British Lion mark and don't serve to vulnerable groups.

Serves 6

Amaretti with Lemon Mascarpone

Hands-on time: 15 minutes
Cooking time: 5 minutes

finely sliced zest and juice of ¼ lemon

1 tbsp golden caster sugar, plus a little extra to sprinkle

50g (2oz) mascarpone cheese

12 amaretti biscuits

1 Put the lemon juice into a small pan. Add the sugar and dissolve over a low heat. Once the sugar has dissolved, add the lemon zest and cook for 1–2 minutes – it will curl up. Using a slotted spoon, lift out the zest strips and lay them on a sheet of baking parchment, putting the syrup to one side. Sprinkle the strips with sugar to coat.

2 Beat the mascarpone in a bowl to soften, then stir in the reserved sugar syrup.

3 Put a blob of mascarpone on each amaretti biscuit, then top with a couple of strips of the crystallised lemon peel.

Perfect Sorbet

Sorbets have a fine, smooth texture and are most frequently fruit-flavoured. Fruits vary in sweetness, so taste the mixture before freezing. Remove the sorbet from the freezer 20 minutes before serving.

Simple orange sorbet

To serve six, you will need:
the zest of 3 oranges and the juice of 6 oranges, about 600ml (1 pint), 200g (7oz) granulated sugar, 1 tbsp orange flower water and 1 medium egg white.

1. Put the orange zest and sugar in a pan with 300ml (½ pint) water. Bring slowly to the boil, stirring. Simmer for 5 minutes, leave to cool for 2 minutes, then strain and cool completely.

2. Strain the orange juice into the syrup and add the orange flower water. Chill for 30 minutes.

3. Using an ice-cream maker, follow the manufacturer's instructions but remove the sorbet halfway through.

4. Whisk the egg white, add to the bowl, and continue churning until the sorbet is firm enough to scoop.

Granitas

Granita is an Italian water ice with larger crystals than a sorbet. It isn't churned but is broken up with a fork, which makes it more like a frozen fruit slush. Quick to melt, it must be served and eaten quickly and makes a wonderful refresher in summer. Fruit-flavoured, granitas are frequently also popularly flavoured with coffee.

Making by hand

1 Pour the mixture into a shallow container, cover and freeze for about 3 hours, until partially frozen to a slushy consistency. Beat the sorbet with a whisk or fork until smooth.

2 Whisk the egg white and fold into the mixture, then return to the freezer and freeze until firm enough to scoop, 2–4 hours.

Tutti Frutti Sorbet

Hands-on time: 5 minutes

450g (1lb) frozen fruit of your choice, such as blueberries, raspberries, summer fruits or mango

75g (3oz) icing sugar

1 tbsp fruit liqueur, such as framboise or cassis, plus extra to drizzle (optional)

chopped nuts, grated chocolate or freshly chopped mint to decorate (optional)

1 Put the frozen fruit and icing sugar into a food processor or blender, pour in the liqueur, if you like, or add 1 tbsp water and whiz for 1–2 minutes until smooth and scoopable. Be patient – it may take a while for the fruit to break up.

2 Spoon the sorbet into bowls or glasses and drizzle with extra liqueur, or decorate with chopped nuts, grated chocolate or mint, if you like. Serve immediately.

FREEZE AHEAD
You can make up batches of sorbet and store in an airtight container in the freezer for up to three months.

Cheat's Baked Alaska

Hands-on time: 10 minutes
Cooking time: about 5 minutes

1 toffee waffle biscuit

500ml tub chocolate ice cream

2 medium egg whites

50g (2oz) caster sugar

SAVE EFFORT

If you get bubbly outcroppings of sugar on your meringues (called weeping), it could mean the sugar was not added gradually enough or that the meringues were baked in an oven that was too hot. If the weeping happens during cooling, the meringues weren't baked for long enough.

1 Preheat the oven to 220°C (200°C fan oven) mark 7. Put the toffee waffle biscuit on a baking tray. Cut the ice cream out of its cardboard tub using scissors and put on top of the biscuit, top down.

2 Put the egg whites into a bowl. Using hand-held electric beaters, whisk the egg whites until they hold stiff peaks. Still whisking constantly, add the sugar – the meringue mixture should be thick and glossy.

3 Use a palette knife to spread meringue over the ice-cream mound, sealing in the ice cream completely. Bake for 3–5 minutes until the meringue is browning. Lift on to a serving plate using the palette knife and serve immediately.

Serves 6

Cheat's Tiramisu

Hands-on time: 15 minutes

375g (13oz) mascarpone cheese

75g (3oz) plain chocolate,
finely chopped

2 medium eggs

75g (3oz) caster sugar

175g–200g (6–7oz) chocolate loaf cake
or brownies, roughly chopped

6 tbsp Tia Maria liqueur

cocoa powder to dust

gold leaf to sprinkle

1 Mix the mascarpone and chocolate together in a large bowl until combined. In a separate medium bowl, beat together the eggs and sugar using hand-held electric beaters for about 5 minutes until pale and moussey. Use a large metal spoon to fold the egg mixture into the mascarpone bowl.

2 Divide half the chocolate loaf cake or brownies among six large glasses, then drizzle ½ tbsp of liqueur into each glass. Next, divide half the mascarpone mixture equally among the glasses. Repeat the layering process once more.

3 Cut a star template from a sheet of paper. Lay over one glass and dust with cocoa powder. Repeat with the remaining glasses and sprinkle gold leaf over each pudding. Serve immediately.

Note: As this pudding contains raw eggs, buy those with the British Lion mark and don't serve to vulnerable groups.

Serves 6

Luscious Lemon Passion Pots

Hands-on time: 5 minutes

150g (5oz) condensed milk

50ml (2fl oz) double cream

grated zest and juice of 1 large lemon

1 passion fruit

1 Put the condensed milk, double cream and lemon zest and juice into a medium bowl and whisk until thick and fluffy. Spoon into two small ramekins or coffee cups and chill until needed – or carry on with the recipe if you can't wait.

2 To serve, halve the passion fruit, scoop out the seeds and use to decorate the lemon pots.

Serves 2

Perfect Chocolate

Chocolate is a delicious dessert ingredient. It also makes great decorations, and a simple sauce with many variations. The type of chocolate you choose will have a dramatic effect on the end product. For the best results, buy chocolate that has a high proportion of cocoa solids, preferably at least 70%.

Chocolate shavings

This is the easiest decoration of all because it doesn't call for melting chocolate. Use chilled chocolate.

1 Hold a chocolate bar upright on a work surface and shave pieces off the edge with a y-shaped vegetable peeler.
2 Alternatively, grate the chocolate against a coarse or medium-coarse grater to make very fine shavings.

Melting

For cooking or making decorations, chocolate is usually melted first.

1 Break the chocolate into pieces and put in a heatproof bowl or in the top of a double boiler. Set over a pan of gently simmering water.
2 Heat very gently until the chocolate starts to melt, then stir only once or twice until completely melted.

1

2

Larger chocolate curls

1 Spread melted chocolate in a thin layer on a marble slab or clean work surface. Leave to firm up.
2 Using a sharp, flat-ended blade (such as a metal pastry scraper), push through the chocolate at a 45-degree angle. The size of the curls will be determined by the width of the blade.

Chocolate sauce

1 Chop plain chocolate (at least 70% cocoa solids) and put it in a saucepan with 50ml (2fl oz) water per 100g (3½oz) chocolate.
2 Heat slowly, allowing the chocolate to melt, then stir until the sauce is smooth.

2

1

Cheat's Chocolate Soufflés

Hands-on time: 15 minutes
Cooking time: about 10–12 minutes

butter to grease

75g (3oz) plain chocolate

225ml (8fl oz) fresh chocolate custard

3 medium egg whites

25g (1oz) caster sugar

icing sugar, to dust

1 Preheat the oven to 220°C (200°C fan oven) mark 7. Put a baking sheet on the middle shelf to heat up, making sure there's enough space for the soufflés to rise. Grease six 125ml (4fl oz) ramekins.

2 Finely grate the chocolate, or whiz until it resembles breadcrumbs. Dust the insides of the ramekins with 25g (1oz) of the chocolate.

3 Mix the custard and remaining chocolate together in a large bowl. In a separate bowl, whisk the egg whites until stiff but not dry, then gradually add the caster sugar to the egg whites, whisking well after each addition. Using a metal spoon, fold the egg whites into the custard mixture.

4 Quickly divide the mixture among the prepared ramekins, put them on to the preheated baking sheet and bake for 10–12 minutes until well risen. Dust the soufflés with icing sugar and serve immediately.

Chocolate-dipped Strawberries

Hands-on time: about 10 minutes, plus chilling
Cooking time: 5 minutes

50g (2oz) white chocolate (milk or plain, if you like), chopped

about 12 strawberries

SAVE EFFORT

Make these chocolate-dipped strawberries a day ahead and store covered in the fridge until needed.

1 Melt the chocolate in a heatproof bowl over a pan of gently simmering water (or blast for 20 seconds in the microwave until it is melted). Meanwhile, wash and thoroughly dry the strawberries, leaving the green hulls on.

2 Holding a strawberry by its hull, dip the fruit into the melted chocolate. Put on to a baking sheet lined with parchment paper. Repeat with each of the remaining berries, then chill to set. Serve the strawberries either chilled or at room temperature.

Makes 12

Calorie Gallery

372 cal ♥ 27g protein
12g fat (4g sat) ♥ 2g fibre
42g carb ♥ 1.7g salt

12

463 cal ♥ 27g protein
17g fat (6g sat) ♥ 8g fibre
52g carb ♥ 1.8g salt

14

373 cal ♥ 24g protein
22g fat (4g sat) ♥ 2g fibre
23g carb ♥ 2.6g salt

16

427 cal ♥ 17g protein
9g fat (2g sat) ♥ 4g fibre
72g carb ♥ 1.6g salt

18

505 cal ♥ 26g protein
16g fat (4g sat) ♥ 3g fibre
54g carb ♥ 0.6g salt

32

440 cal ♥ 10g protein
12g fat (8g sat) ♥ 3g fibre
68g carb ♥ 2.8g salt

36

564 calories ♥ 24g protei
21g fat (12g sat) ♥ 4g fibr
66g carb ♥ 1.0g salt

38

363 cal ♥ 5g protein
7g fat (1g sat) ♥ 1g fibre
69g carb ♥ 0.5g salt

58

502 cal ♥ 38g protein
26g fat (17g sat) ♥ 3g fibre
27g carb ♥ 0.4g salt

60

511 cal ♥ 35g protein
13g fat (3g sat) ♥ 4g fibr
66g carb ♥ 1.1g salt

62

334 cal ♥ 11g protein
22g fat (6g sat) ♥ 1g fibre
25g carb ♥ 1.5g salt

74

600 cal ♥ 11g protein
37g fat (11g sat) ♥ 4g fibre
57g carb ♥ 1.0g salt

76

per tbsp. 65 cal ♥ 1g protein
3g fat (2g sats) ♥ 0g fibre
10g carb ♥ 0.1g salt

78

406 cal ♥ 29g protein
32g fat (12g sat) ♥ 1g fib
2g carb ♥ 2.8g salt

84

420 cal ♥ 19g protein
3g fat (2g sat) ♥ 2g fibre
71g carb ♥ 0.8g salt

447 cal ♥ 18g protein
7g fat (3g sat) ♥ 4g fibre
82g carb ♥ 1.9g salt

449 cal ♥ 21g protein
40g fat (19g sat) ♥ 0g fibre
1g carb ♥ 1g salt

429 cal ♥ 28g protein
20g fat (11g sat) ♥ 0.2g fibre
38g carb ♥ 3.1g salt

330 cal ♥ 21g protein
3g fat (14g sat) ♥ 2g fibre
10g carb ♥ 0.5g salt

282 cal ♥ 21g protein
15g fat (3g sat) ♥ 3g fibre
16g carb ♥ 0.4g salt

508 cal ♥ 29g protein
19g fat (11g sat)
3g fibre ♥ 64g carb ♥ 1.9g salt

857 cal ♥ 34g protein
51g fat (6g sat) ♥ 4g fibre
67g carb ♥ 1.6g salt

750 cal ♥ 30g protein
38g fat (12g sat) ♥ 3g fibre
74g carb ♥ 2.2g salt

270 cal ♥ 34g protein
10g fat (3g sat) ♥ 6g fibre
12g carb ♥ 0.3g salt

544 cal ♥ 14g protein
33g fat (17g sat) ♥ 1g fibre
31g carb ♥ 1.6g salt

442 cal ♥ 38g protein
15g fat (5g sat) ♥ 4g fibre
41g carb ♥ 0.7g salt

396 cal ♥ 44g protein
2g fat (7g sat) ♥ 0.8g fibre
6g carb ♥ 0.6g salt

(without bun) 253 cal
8g protein ♥ 18g fat (3g sat)
1g fibre ♥ 16g carb ♥ 0.8g salt

655 cal ♥ 50g protein
23g fat (9g sat) ♥ 4g fibre
69g carb ♥ 0.5g salt

625 cal ♥ 63g protein
33g fat (17g sat) ♥ 1g fibre
20g carb ♥ 4.8g salt

20

22

26

30

2

46

48

50

64

66

68

70

36

88

90

92

298 cal ♥ 7g protein
21g fat (11g sat) ♥ 2g fibre
20g carb ♥ 0.7g salt

94

650 cal ♥ 59g protein
37g fat (18g sat) ♥ 2g fibre
39g carb ♥ 1.3g salt

96

365 cal ♥ 31g protein
13g fat (3g sat) ♥ 2g fibre
34g carb ♥ 0.7g salt

100

475 cal ♥ 18g protein
40g fat (7g sat) ♥ 3g fibre
10g carb ♥ 1.5g salt

102

298 cal ♥ 17g protein
22g fat (11g sat) ♥ 4g fibre
9g carb ♥ 1.4g salt

112

282 cal ♥ 27g protein
11g fat (2g sat) ♥ 2.7g fibre
27g carb ♥ 3.3g salt

116

373 cal ♥ 42g protein
16g fat (8g sat) ♥ 0.4g fibre
15g carb ♥ 0.8g salt

118

496 cal ♥ 24g protein
17g fat (7g sat) ♥ 7g fibre
65g carb ♥ 2.5g salt

120

370 cal ♥ 35g protein
8g fat (2g sat) ♥ 3g fibre
41g carb ♥ 1.8g salt

132

484 cal ♥ 24g protein
42g fat (20g sat) ♥ 0g fibre
1g carb ♥ 0.4g salt

134

365 cal ♥ 15g protein
9g fat (5g sat) ♥ 3g fibre
59g carb ♥ 0.3g salt

136

369 cal ♥ 27g protein
25g fat (9g sat) ♥ 2g fibre
10g carb ♥ 0.9g salt

138

180 cal ♥ 1g protein
8g fat (4g sat) ♥ 0.2g fibre
28g carb ♥ 0.4g salt

152

(using liqueur): 110 cal
1g protein ♥ 0.1g fat (0g sat)
3g fibre ♥ 27g carb ♥ 0g salt

156

231 calories ♥ 5g protein
11g fat (7g sat) ♥ 0.2g fibre
28g carb ♥ 0.3g salt

158

614 cal ♥ 7g protein
43g fat (23g sat) ♥ 0.3g fibre
45g carb ♥ 0.9g salt

160

736 cal ♥ 28g protein
g fat (25g sat) ♥ 2g fibre
58g carb ♥ 1.2g salt

04

775 cal ♥ 69g protein
41g fat (16g sat) ♥ 2.5g fibre
59g carb ♥ 1.0g salt

106

(without cream): 566 cal
48g protein ♥ 12g fat (5g sat)
3g fibre ♥ 71g carb ♥ 1.1g salt

108

471 cal ♥ 14g protein
29g fat (9g sat) ♥ 6g fibre
38g carb ♥ 3.0g salt

110

): 861 cal ♥ 29g protein
fat (35g sat) ♥ 2g fibre
49g carb ♥ 3.0g salt

6): 574 cal ♥ 19g protein
fat (23g sat) ♥ 1g fibre
33g carb ♥ 2.0g salt

2

386 calories ♥ 12g protein
6g fat (1g sat) ♥ 4g fibre
72g carb ♥ 1.5g salt

124

524 cal ♥ 35g protein
31g fat (12g sat) ♥ 7g fibre
29g carb ♥ 1.8g salt

126

583 cal ♥ 34g protein
30g fat (15g sat) ♥ 4g fibre
45g carb ♥ 1.2g salt

128

647 cal ♥ 34g protein
44g fat (23g sat) ♥ 1g fibre
33g carb ♥ 1.0g salt

40

677 cal ♥ 29g protein
24g fat (9g sat) ♥ 4g fibre
87g carb ♥ 2.0g salt

142

616 cal ♥ 5.5g protein
35g fat (9g sat) ♥ 1g fibre
30g carb ♥ 1.5g salt

144

654 cal ♥ 9g protein
52g fat (33g sat) ♥ 0.5g fibre
40g carb ♥ 0.3g salt

150

377 cal ♥ 7g protein
g fat (13g sat) ♥ 0.3g fibre
43g carb ♥ 0.3g salt

62

126 cal ♥ 3g protein
5g fat (2g sat) ♥ 0.4g fibre
19g carb ♥ 0.1g salt

166

per dipped strawberry:
27 cal ♥ 0.4g protein
1g fat (1g sats) ♥ 0.1g fibre
4g carb ♥ 0g salt

168

Index

PICTURE CREDITS

Photographers: Steve Baxter (13, 15, 17, 19, 21, 23, 33, 37, 39, 47, 59, 61, 63, 65, 67, 69, 71, 75 and 77); Nicki Dowey (page 27); William Lingwood (page 165L); Gareth Morgans (pages 43, 79 and 157); Myles New (pages 85, 87, 89, 91, 93, 95, 97, 101, 103, 105, 107, 109, 111, 113, 117, 11-, 121, 123, 125, 127, 129, 133, 135, 137, 139, 141, 143, 145 and 161); Craig Robertson (pages 44, 45, 51, 153, 154, 155, 164 and 165R); Lucinda Symons (pages 31 and 49); Philip Webb (page 151); Kate Whitaker (pages 159, 163, 167 and 169); Rachel Whiting (front cover).

Home Economists:
Joanna Farrow, Emma Jane Frost, Teresa Goldfinch, Alice Hart, Lucy McKelvie, Kim Morphew, Bridget Sargeson and Mari Mereid Williams.

Stylists: Tamzin Ferdinando, Wei Tang, Helen Trent and Fanny Ward.

BAKE ME A CAKE
There's always time for cake

EASY PEASY MEALS
Easy meals for every day

LET'S DO BRUNCH
Mouth-watering meals to start your day

CHEAP EATS
Budget-busting ideas that won't break the

SALAD DAYS
Oh-so-fresh ideas for fabulous salads

Available online
and
from all good bookshops

POSH NOSH
Delicious recipes to impress your guest

PARTY FOOD
Delicious recipes to get the party started

SLOW STOPPERS
Slow-cooked meals packed with flavour

GREAT VEG
Inspired ideas for delicious veggie meals

AL FRESCO EATS
Easy grills, barbecues and picnics

ROAST IT
There's nothing better than a delicious roast

FLASH IN THE PAN
Spice up your noodles and stir-fries

GLUTEN-FREE AND EASY
Oh-so-good-for-you recipes that taste great

LOW FAT LOW CAL
Nice recipes don't need to be naughty